The Rapid Entrepreneur!

How To Quit Your Job And Start A Business! From Idea Generation To Launch!

The Entrepreneur's guide to starting a successful business

Neil "Snowy" Phillips

TABLE OF CONTENTS

Introduction

I'd like to thank you for taking this opportunity to own this course and the information contained within. Apologies in advance for writing style of this course, it is a little "clunky" As I was more concerned with getting the information out there rather than making it polished and perfect. As the old expression goes and it's something that all entrepreneurs can learn you don't have to get it perfect you just have to get going.. Before I get into the meat of it, I'd like to tell you about how the course came about. Originally, the question was brought up in a meeting where there was a professor of entrepreneurship asking, "Can you teach entrepreneurship?"

I have spent many years as what I would regard a serial entrepreneur. I am a person who has started and both succeeded and failed in many business ventures. I thought about the question, and I thought about it sincerely. The professor of entrepreneurship who was giving the lecture that evening was just that, a *professor* of entrepreneurship. He had never started a business, never succeeded in a business, never failed in a business. He was just teaching a subject on which I felt he was ill-qualified to actually have an opinion. He dropped a lot of names, but other than that, his ideas seemed very text-book, and not real-world tested. That evening, I got home and I thought about the subject a bit more. "Can you actually teach entrepreneurship? Is that a possibility?"

Those who have done can teach!

I started thinking about how I developed the businesses I started in the past, and tried to put together a framework that would take most of the risk out of starting an entrepreneurial venture. Let's be honest, most people who get into business go about it the wrong way. So, with this course, this manual, I've put together what I consider to be a strategy that eliminates the risk, or at least some of the risk, of starting an entrepreneurial venture. It will allow you to know, within reason, whether the venture you're starting has a great possibility to succeed.

I will also state that my process of entrepreneurship is not the *only* process; it does preclude some areas of entrepreneurship. However, I do believe that this process will allow the average person the opportunity to find a business, a vehicle to actually earn money. If you are trying to get into a business of your own, this process will allow you to see if there is a market for your business. Before you invest any real amount of money, it will help you to generate ideas for your business. It will help you to obtain the resources for your business and it will help you to actually bring the business to market. This course will demonstrate how to market a new business in an effective way that will give you the best chance of making your business work.

My system is a holistic system. It takes you through all the areas I believe need to be accomplished in order to get a business off the ground, growing and running.

GET YOUR FREE REPORT NOW:

10 Ways to generate a million dollar idea in 60 seconds!

Actually before we continue I think it would really help if you could start getting ready to come up with some really great business ideas. This will prepare your mind for the rest of the course. So Quick stop reading and head over to

http://thesnowhow.com/yourfreereport/

Go Get It NOW! Really It Will Help!

About a man

Before we go any further, what qualifies me to teach any of this? I started my first entrepreneurial endeavors at a very young age. From 14 onwards, I started coming up with business ideas. By the time I reached 30 I had managed to have 3 or 4 of my ideas come to fruition and, have more than enough passive income to cover my needs. I haven't worked a hard day in about ten years. Many of my friends describe my lifestyle as the equivalent to Hugh Grant's character in *About A Boy*. I'm schedule-free. I do what I want, with whomever I want, when I want. I travel where I want. I eat where I want. My time is my own.

If you asked any of my friends what I'm like as a human being, they'd probably tell you I'm very laid back. This doesn't make me a good person. I don't tell you this to impress you, I tell you this to impress *upon* you that if you are even remotely enthusiastic about doing what you do, you can far surpass anything I've ever done.

I've had to learn a lot of the information I'm passing on to you through trial and error. I went to the school of hard knocks, and often used strategies that didn't work. Eventually I formulated a system that perpetually works with nearly every idea I have. My ideas tend to work with far more frequency than they did when I originally started out on my journey of entrepreneurship.

I'm not the richest person in the world. I don't count myself in the super-rich category. But I am in a situation that, by anyone's yardstick, is comfortable. I'm 41 years old and my time is my own. If that sounds like something that would be of interest to you, keep reading. Hopefully along the way you'll come up with some ideas that will fast-track you on your way to where I am at this moment. And those of you who are super-motivated and super-committed to getting what you want will far outshine anything I've ever done. Thank you.

Chapter 1

Choosing the Right Vehicle

Before you get started in any business, you need to find the right vehicle. Your vehicle will be the type of business you choose to start. Within any marketplace, there are many vehicles. Some vehicles are better than others, but making sure you are in the right business for you is most important. When determining the vehicle that fits your life best, you have to know a bit about yourself. Clearly I used the word vehicle there a lot. I will explain more shortly.

Are You Ready?

If you have time pressures, family pressures or other obligations, you can't exactly go after a business that will consume all your time or take time away from what's important to you. You should be very clear about any business idea you have: how much time you're going to devote to it, how much effort you're going to devote to it, and any parties that may be affected by your getting into that business (family, friends etc.) You have to be very clear that the parties affected are on board with your endeavor.

If you are going to make a business go and grow, you have to find the right vehicle for the right 'you' at the time you begin to undertake it. Let's say you are in the process of having a baby and you recognise that that will be the focus of your attention and take up most of your time. It may not the right time for you to be starting a business that may take up your every waking hour. Even if it isn't a new family member, maybe you have other obligations, other things in mind, other challenges or situations that you have to overcome. You need to make sure that you are starting a business at the right time for you.

If you try to start a project but the timing is all off, this will do more damage to you and your long-term business endeavors than anything else. Timing is all important when you are getting involved in a new venture. You must be honest with yourself and decide whether you have the time it takes to develop, coordinate and run your business. If you do realize that you have time constraints, maybe you should look for a vehicle that will be appropriate to start your first entrepreneurial endeavour. Fear not there are lots of ways to start different businesses with limited time. Granted that the more time you have the better it will be for you, but don't let limited time put you off. You will just have to buckle up and knuckle down.

Knowing is Half the Battle

It also helps to have knowledge of your vehicle before undertaking it as a business venture. If you don't have a basic education in that field, it does not give you the best chance of your being able to start a business in a specified technical field. For example, a gardener wouldn't be the ideal person to go off and start a business in genetic engineering or rocket design.

That said, it is possible to find a business and not have all the knowledge required to run it on your own. I will show you later strategies to quickly gain the knowledge you need for any business from others. Bear in mind, that to run a business endeavor, you will need the right knowledge at some stage.

Sometimes, you will be able to get into a business that has already been established. In this case, most of the ground-work has already been laid for you. By following trends within the business market, you might be able to find a business that has the potential to earn far greater profits than it has already. It has come of age. It's the business's time. Sometimes, you can make money with very little skill or talent for business just by being wise enough to position yourself on the front of a coming business wave. We will talk a bit more about doing that in the section on idea generation.

All You Need is Love

I would also suggest that you do what you love to do. It's not always necessary that you are involved in a business that you love, but it certainly helps. Sometimes a business can go and grow even if you have no love for it. However, that situation is very rare and having no love, being indifferent or hating a business makes it much harder to start.

You should do what you love to do for several reasons. Firstly, if you are starting to grow a business you will spend many hours doing so. If you are doing something you don't like the propensity will be there for you to give up that business before it actually gets off the ground. Sometimes when the business is starting out hard times set upon you, it begins to take up all of your time, and you don't see much reward for your efforts. If you do not love what you are doing, there will be a part of you that wants to quit. If you love what you're doing, no matter how hard it gets, no matter the hardships and the problems that you face, you will have that extra incentive to continue onwards.

Secondly, you will have to convince people-- investors, bankers, customers-- that your product or service is worthwhile. If they can see the enthusiasm you have for your business because you love it, they are more likely to trust you. This makes the sales process far easier. When venturing out on your own in business, you will likely have to convince spouses, partners, friends and family members that you are doing the right thing. If they can see that you love what you are doing and are truly passionate about your project, you are far more likely to garner support than if you were doing something just for the sake of the money.

For the Love of Money

I am not saying that doing something for the sake of the money is necessarily a bad thing. I have successfully started businesses when I have absolutely no interest in the market whatsoever. It is possible to do. If that is the case, however, you still need to show your investors that you have enthusiasm and passion for the business. They are more likely to trust you than if you seem to genuinely not care.

As with anything in life, actually loving something is much easier than faking it. Do your best to find a vehicle that suits you, your current situation in life and your passions.

Chapter 2

Finding Your Marketplace

One of the best bits of business advice you will ever get comes courtesy of the late genius Gary Halbert. For those of you who don't know of him, he was a fantastic teacher, copywriter and all around unbelievable business brain. One day he was giving a lecture on marketing and he asked this question, "If you and I both owned restaurants and we were in a contest to see who could outcompete the other, what one advantage would you most like to have on your side to help you win? You may have any advantage you ask for, and I only want one single advantage for myself." Some said they wanted the best food, best location, some said a McDonalds franchise, some said the cheapest prices, some said the best chefs and the list went on. Eventually, after everyone finished giving their opinions, a lot of which would sound like reasonable and practical ideas to have the best restaurant, Gary said that what he wanted, for his restaurant to perpetually outcompete the other, was a starving crowd with money.

Anyone Hungry?

Now think about that for a second, what he's saying is that what you want for your business are people who want your product and have money to pay for it. As silly as that sounds, that is the key component to all business. If you are going to be in a business, you want people who want your products or service to such a degree that they are actually willing to spend their own money to get it. Gary recognized this, and the simplicity of his statement does not undermine its genius. If you can find a starving crowd, find out what they want and deliver it to them, then to be quite honest, you're halfway to getting your business off the ground.

So, when you're thinking about a business, you need to be asking the questions: Who are my customers? Where are they? How can I find them?

How can I easily find them and cost-efficiently find them? And what do they want? If you know there is marketplace, a niche that's there to be served, a customer base that's looking for your product, (problem that you solve, desire that you meet) what exactly do they want? Do they have a specific interest?

Above Par

Let's say for example that you decide to get involved in a market. Well you'd go to the that market, and ask them what problems they have. What needs to be solved? Once they've told you what they want, you're almost there. The next step is finding a way to deliver that to them. The next question after that is, if you know what they want and where they are, how much are they prepared to pay for a solution to their problem? So you need to find and develop strategies to enable you to find out if your market is prepared to pay for your product. How do you do this…. You ask them! Most people skip this step and it is one of the all time cardinal sins of business. Most people who fail in business skip this step. So be warned.

An awful lot of people make the mistake of getting into a business where they have found a marketplace, found what they want, and although the people seem to be enthusiastic about the item, they are not ready to reach in their pocket and pay money for it. Many inventors encounter this problem. They find a unique and clever solution to a problem that everyone says is a good idea, but no one is actually prepared to take money out of their pocket and actually purchase from you. All the inventor has left is an idea.

Love Hurts

This can be a very, very costly method for starting a business, and unfortunately, a lot of people still do it. They come up with a great idea, and they fall in love with their idea, which usually is a mistake. They fall in love with their idea, they fall in love with their product, they fall in love with their service, they fall in love with the idea of their business, but what they fail to do is *fall in love with their marketplace*.

They should fall in love with their customers and what their customers want. They should find out everything they can about their customers: where they are, what they want and how much they'll pay. One of the simplest and most cost-effective ways to do this is to test. How do you test I hear you ask? Well there are a number of way. Test where your market place is, test how easily they are accessible, and test how much they're willing to pay. This can be done by contacting them directly through the various sources that we'll talk about later in the book: by phone, word of mouth, simple advertisements or direct mail or more reasonably and quickly now using the power of the internet through groups and other places that your "crowed" hangs out. So find a group of people, find out what their problems are, and as long as you find that the people are easily accessible, then you may be on your way to finding a reasonable market.

What you're looking for as well is accessibility of the marketplace. Suppose you could find a great market, and the market is people who are interested in the migratory habits of seabirds. The people who are interested in this subject are absolutely ravenous about the subject, so passionate about it that they are willing to spend an awful lot of money on it. But if you can't reach these people, in an easily affordable and effective manner, then the marketplace is useless to you.

Once you have a starving crowd with a ravenous passion or reasonable problem they want solved quickly or a burning desire for something that they absolutely must have, then you will have a massive advantage over people who have fallen in love with their product or service and not fallen in love with their market place.

After You

When developing a new business, you may hear that you must be the first person in the market. Sometimes, blazing the trail can be incredibly profitable. But the upside potential is not always in proportion to the downside risk of being the first into a marketplace.

More often than not, it's far better to let another person test the waters for you, make all the mistakes, and either fail in that market or succeed in that market the hard way. A lot of times, even when they fail in the market, you can look from an outside perspective, see what they've done wrong, correct their mistakes, and basically take their concept without the mistakes and use it to your advantage.

Never Ask Kevin Costner for Business Advice

Before I go any further, I must expose a myth a lot of business people's fall for, the 'build it and they will come' mentality. (This pertains to the necessity of the market's being easily reachable that I mentioned earlier.) You may have seen the fantastic film *Field of Dreams* in which Kevin Costner builds a baseball field in the middle of his corn crop for no good reason, and eventually, "if you build it, they will come," people turn up, just to sit happily and look at his baseball field. A lot of people who are starting businesses, especially new businesses, untried and untested, seem to think that if they build it, people will automatically find their way to the business with a big bag of money ready to buy the new product or service. I can assure you that this is just not the case.

If you develop the best new widget you are not guaranteed business. Sometimes even if you have the best product or the best service or the best idea out there, people *won't* just come knocking on your door. It is a myth that has caused more heartbreak than anything else. So before you even start a project, more than anything else, you have to find a starving crowd with an irrational passion for what you're offering, and they've got to be easily reachable.

If your potential customers don't have those three important characteristics: they are ravenously starving for your product, they are prepared to pay money for it and they are easily reachable, then I advise the new entrepreneur: abandon your idea.

Look I'm not saying it is not possible to develop the new new things, it is. I'm just saying that more often than not new entrepreneurs get totally run over when they are looking to go down this route. You've been warned.

The Lonesome Road

As I mentioned at the very start of the program, I teach is what I call a holistic system. That is to say, it was not suggested that this is a complete system of entrepreneurship. As I mentioned, people have done the exact opposite of what I advise and succeeded. They have come up with a product or service, come up with a brilliant idea, and have gone off without an easily definable marketplace, and made absolute fortunes. It is possible to do that. That is the reality. But for every one person who succeeds going down that route and making their fortune in that marketplace by blazing a trail, there are hundreds upon hundreds who have fallen by the wayside. They've had their dreams of becoming the next multimillionaire or of growing their business to build themselves the lifestyle they had always wanted ripped away from them.

The road to success of every endeavor is paved with the blood, sweat and tears of those who have failed to do it by trying to blaze a solitary trail. It is possible, but it is not, in my opinion, the best way to go about starting a business. What I have tried to do with this course is build a process that allows you the best and most reasonable chance to get into your own business successfully.

In summary, when you're looking to get into a business, the first thing you want to do is find a marketplace, a starving crowd. Look for people who have a rabid interest in something, a problem that they absolutely want solved, or people who seem unreasonably interested in a singular area. When you have that, you are most of the way to getting a business going and growing.

Some of the areas with irrational passions and a proven marketplace include the diet and fitness industries, the health industry, the business opportunity industry, helping people save money, improving credit, business to business sales and marketing, business opportunities, investing and trading, real estate buying and selling, sex and relationships. Just take a look at your local magazine rack, and see all the hobbies and interests that are available there for ideas about what people are interested in. You may want to look on the internet, using search terms like "how to" or " learn" to find out what people are interested in doing. Look for problems. Keep your ears open. Someone once told me, 'keep your money goggles open.' Everything you see out there is an opportunity. I'll talk more later on about finding business ideas, but first find your starving crowd.

Chapter 3

Idea Generation Part One: Observation

In this next section, I'll be teaching you some strategies I use for generating ideas. Despite what many people new to business think, ideas are not the "be all and end all" of a business endeavor. You can come up with a million $/£ idea every second of every day. I have had many people come up to me with ideas they say will be worth millions, but often they fail to do anything with them. Most people fail when they try to implement their ideas. Actually speaking of ideas I heard someone say recently to someone when they said they had an idea for a mobile app "Yep and I have an idea my app will solve all of everyone in the worlds problems. Come back when you have something concrete". So an idea in and of itself is worthless.

That being said, being able to develop a consistent series of ideas that will enable you to make money is a useful ability to have. In this section I will show you some techniques that will allow you to develop a stream of good, solid, business ideas. These techniques will allow you to come up with plans and strategies to test a business for yourself. In the future you will be able to use these techniques to grow and consistently improve your business.

The idea generation section is one of the cornerstones of my system. Although idea generation is a multi-faceted subject with many sub-sections, many people give it more weight than it deserves. When you are finished reading this section, you will understand that people come up with great ideas every day. The problems they face are often in the implementation of those ideas.

A side not yo should get into the habit of coming up with 10 new ideas each and every day. If you do this you will strengthen your idea muscle. This will allow you not to be hooked on a single idea and be too invested in it. Because you no longer at the mercy of one ideaitis you will be free to concentrate on looking for the best idea you have not the first idea you have. If you do this every day for a year you will in effect have 3650 ideas a reasonable person would realise that there has to be more than a few good ones in there.

Anyway lets get on with idea generation.

Focus Your Money Goggles

The first way to generate ideas is to keep your eyes and ears open and become a problem solver. Problems often translate into great business opportunities. Wherever you are, at the office, walking down the street, sitting in the bar/coffee shop: listen to other people's conversations. Human beings have an inordinate amount of talent for complaining about stuff. The majority of people's complaints aren't reasonable or rational, but on occasion people will give you ideas or opportunities by saying something like, "Do you know what someone should do? They should invent . . . ." or, "I wish one day someone could sort out this [whatever.]" I have been literally walking down the street and seen ideas that later got turned into businesses.

For example, a few years ago I saw a woman pushing a baby carriage in the rain. She had a shopping bag in one hand and an umbrella in the other and seemed to be having difficulty juggling the three. I thought to myself at the time, "They should make an umbrella attachment for carriages, wheelchairs and prams so that they and the umbrella would function as one, thus solving this particular problem." I thought about it and never did anything. A couple of years later I saw that someone had invented that solution and was obviously selling it. Like I say, problems come in all shapes and forms, so whenever you see a problem, don't think of it as an obstacle; think of it as an opportunity. As a potential entrepreneur, you should always be asking the questions: How can I solve people's problems? How can I make life easier for people? How can I make things faster and more efficient?

There's Always Room for Improvement

The second strategy for developing an idea is to improve an existing product. If you can improve something that already exists, your new product will already have a proven market, so you're not going to be reinventing the wheel. If you look around an average space such as a home or office, you can observe its objects. There are 1001 objects that people are already buying, so if you can find a way to improve those objects, you don't have to worry about finding new customers. Think how many times people have improved the standard corkscrew to open wine bottles, or the countless different varieties of chairs, tables, lights etc. If you can improve something that has a natural market already in place, selling your product becomes much easier.

The Times They Are a Changin'

The next idea generation concept is utilizing the natural progression of change in the world. Changes occur in various categories, and anytime there's a change there's a new opportunity. The most apparent of these categories is probably the change in technology. Over the last 20 or 30 years the people who have made the big money have seen a change in technology and jumped at the opportunity it offered. This goes against my "Don't be the first into a market," adage, but using the changes in the field of technology can lead to great business opportunities. Many people have made great fortunes by marketing new products that go along with technology such as the Internet and mobile phones. Every time there is a change in technology, an opportunity arises to earn a great deal of money by getting in there and marketing effectively.

Technology changes all the time. Fifteen years ago, who would have thought that almost every person in the Western world would have a mobile phone in their pocket? That you could take pictures with that mobile phone? That you could surf the internet with that mobile phone? That you could, instead of speaking to people on that phone, spend half the day texting or surfing or putting status updates on Facebook? That for many people it is now their main computer. As you can see, change in technology always creates opportunities. If you can find a way to ride the crest of that wave, there are a lot of options for entrepreneurial enterprise.

Another opportunity-creating change is the change in social interests. Look at how often the needs of your fellow people change. Social interests can include hobbies and trends. Think about dieting or exercise trends. At one stage jogging was all the rage, then gym memberships, followed by yoga, pilates, yogalates, p90x, insanity, cross fit, you get the idea. If you can see habits or social interests changing and get involved in a business near the start of that change, there is always money to be had.

The last type of change I will discuss is change in laws. When there is a law change, there is often an opportunity for someone to make money off of it. In the U.K. and elsewhere it is no longer legal to smoke in public places such as pubs, restaurants or any form of public transportation. I personally haven't profited off of this law change, but if you ask yourself a number of questions, I'm sure you could find ways to make money out of it. The pub and bar economy has been hurt due to many smokers deciding they would rather stay at home to drink. Maybe you could come up with and market ideas that would entice smokers back into the pubs.

Since people who want to smoke now have to go outside, you could find a reasonable way to keep people warm and sheltered so that they feel less like outcasts while they are smoking. Since people have to put cigarettes out somewhere, outdoor ashtrays are becoming more prevalent. In and around the U.K., I have seen all sorts of wall-based ashtrays outside pubs and other non-smoking establishments. Somebody made money off of that change in law. They probably sold very few of those ashtrays up until the law change, but now, I'm sure that many of these innovative ashtrays are sold. The lesson to be taken here is to be aware of changes in the law and ask yourself what sort of opportunities these changes create.

Since I first wrote this section the we have seen the rise of the E-Cigarette. See opportunities are always there.

Your Modeling Career

The next method of developing ideas is quite simple and probably the most effective strategy for developing a business model that works. Model someone else's ideas. Find a business that is already working, take that business's model, adopt it, make it your own, and change it slightly so you don't get sued. The reason to model someone else's business is that it is already proven to work. Beware of the business that looks as if it's a great idea from the outside, but isn't actually profitable. One of the ways to avoid adopting a model that's not working is to look for expansion. If you can see a business that is going and, more importantly, *growing*, then you know it's a successful business model to copy.

Use the successful business's blueprint to adopt every idea that you see is working for them. Adopt their tactics, strategy, marketing, and look. Adopt their methods for finding and bringing in customers, suppliers and distributors. If you can find some ways to improve upon that blueprint, then do so.

One thing to consider when copying someone else's business model is the lag time it would take for that business to expand into your region. You must be able to set up your business before the existing business becomes your competition. Some successful business modeling examples include coffee shop chains and pizza and burger joints that have been modeled after those in the U.S. and re-created in other countries. Companies have also managed to capitalize on a fad, making a fortune by producing the same product in regions the fad had not yet reached. If you travel around the world and keep your eyes open you will see many opportunities caused simply by lag time.

Look for an idea or strategy that is working in another place, possibly in a different region within your own country. Take that model. Take it back to your location and start afresh from there. You know that you have a potential winner of a business idea when you model a business that is already successful.

Chapter 4

Idea Generation Part Two: The Niche

A niche (pronounced neesh not nich as most Americans do) is a special area of demand for a particular product or service. Finding your "starving crowd" is of primary importance, and by clearly defining the group of people who make up that starving crowd, you greatly increase your chance of success. This is called niche marketing. There are many niches within the business world. I am going to teach you about various niche categories that I find particularly important to know, including nostalgia, usage, demographics and price.

A Classic Never Really Goes Out of Style

The first niche I will discuss is one you have definitely noticed already, and that is resurrecting the old. When you resurrect the old, you take products or styles that have lost their market through time, and reintroduce them to a new generation. Examples of this niche can be seen in clothing fashions, architecture and furniture. An example of a successful resurrection of an old product is the new craze in the U.K. for '70s-style digital watches. The old classics now have a new market. The fashion industry is constantly looking back to the past for ideas. Bellbottoms, originally popular in the late '60s and '70s experienced a resurgence in the late 1990s. This works the same for styles of furniture. People are starting to recreate art-deco style furniture and Georgian furniture.

In addition to resurrecting old products and styles, old processes can also be resurrected with much success. In the construction industry, people are starting to look back at how things were made historically. These processes have a value. Some people are demanding old style processes rather than processes we get in today's world. For example, the modern method of furniture manufacturing uses pressed particle board covered in wood veneer, but a high demand has developed for old-style solid wood construction. Older processes for home construction are also now in demand.

Pay attention to the opportunities nostalgia offers. People are awfully nostalgic about bygone eras. Every era has something to offer to the idea-seeking entrepreneur. Each decade in the 20th century is associated with particular fashions, styles of furniture and other products unique to those times. You can even look for ideas from further back in history to the Victorian age, Elizabethan Age, or Georgian Age. There are even niches based solely around nostalgia. I'm not saying that if you are a bike manufacturer people will necessarily want to start riding penny-farthings again, but who knows? There is certainly a market for old toys and games so maybe.

A little research may find you a goldmine in the form of an idea that may have been before it's time when originally created. Joseph Pilates, the man who invented the Pilates system, was around in the 1920s. He invented a lot of exercise machines back then that are wildly popular now. It's the 21st century and people are quite successfully manufacturing and marketing machines Pilates invented almost 100 years ago.

Usage Change

The next important aspect of using niches is to expand the marketplace of an existing product. Many products have made the transition from industrial applications to home consumer use. Examples of some of these products include air conditioning, the internet and various software products. Air conditioning was originally, I believe, designed for industrial use to keep temperatures cool in warehouses, and some bright person said, "Maybe I could make that for the home." Many, many businesses are profiting because of that one thought.

The internet was a classic military application that is now a consumer application. People are using software like Photoshop to modify their family photos, when it was originally an industry application. The microwave, once an industrial product, is now in virtually every kitchen. Perhaps you could even reverse that concept and market something originally intended for consumers to different industries. Ask yourself the question, "What do I see every day that could be used in or by a different marketplace?" If you constantly consider that question, you will undoubtedly come up with some marketable ideas.

It All Depends How You Use It

Another creative way to utilize niches is by expanding the usage of an existing product. Some examples within the idea of usage change include the umbrella/parasol, ski/water-ski and parachute/paraglider. One day the umbrella became a parasol, so instead of providing shelter from the rain it was used to provide shelter from the sun. The ski, originally meant for the snow, is now also used on water. The parachute and hang-glider, used to ease falls from great heights are now also, in the guise of para-gliders and para-sails, use to gain altitude, the opposite use.

Consider the George Forman Grill, clearly a very successful product. Essentially, it is a sandwich toaster (or panini maker) that has been slightly tilted so that grease drains from the food. George changed the use of the original machine from pressing sandwiches to cooking lean steaks and sold millions. I recently heard that he had earned a reported $120+ million from the product. Finding new uses for old products can be very profitable.

Power to the People

You can market your product or service toward different niches of people by using demographic analysis. Demographics are segments of human populations broken down by specific characteristics, such as age, ethnicity, job status, relationship status, et cetera. The more effectively you can target your product or service to a specific demographic niche, the more successful it will be. Also, the more defined your niche is, the more you can charge for your product or service. Large companies often overlook small niches, so smaller entrepreneurs can particularly benefit from this practice.

Some examples of demographic niches by age are teenagers, twentysomethings, middle agers or the elderly. You could also denominate the niche by gender, ethnicity or geographic region. A great example of people who have used specific demographic niches to market their products successfully are Mark Victor Hansen and Jack Canfield, the writers of the *Chicken Soup for the Soul* series. The initial book and its first sequel were so successful that they decided to create volumes specialized to particular demographic niches. They began with *Chicken Soup for the Teenage Soul*, followed by one for the mother's soul, the uncle's soul, the horse rider's soul the golfers soul . . . you get the idea.

If you start studying the different niches for people, you discover that their hobbies, leisure activities and athletic pursuits all define separate marketable groups.   Just go to a bookstore or a library and look at the selection there. Look at magazine racks. Magazines and television shows are terrific examples of products tailored to specific demographic niches. When you look at the products or services advertised in a magazine, you will notice that they are aimed at the same niche as the magazine itself. Being part of a specific niche is something that makes people feel special, so they are more likely to buy things that identify with them personally. The more specifically you can design your product to fit a particular niche, the more market activity and more profit there tends to be.

The Price is Right

Another easily definable niche to consider is the price niche. There are two major price distinctions, the low cost, or "budget" niche and the high cost, or "luxury" niche. When you start a business, consider which of these you want to target.

Some companies make their business out of selling only budget niche products. The furniture store IKEA, the low-cost airline EasyJet, and the clothing store H&M are all prime examples of businesses that cater to the budget niche. Another example of using a low cost strategy is supermarkets' use of own-brand items. They are the cheapest items in the grocery store, all bearing the name of the store. A method sometimes employed by businesses in the budget niche is volume. If they can sell a great deal of something at a low cost, the profit it is in the volume rather than the initial transaction. This is not really the route that I myself prefer, but a lot of businesses go that route. You could also offer the lowest price as a loss-leader, which I will explain in further detail later.

One thing I must say is that if you are going to offer a very low cost product, you need to be careful. In order to make sure your customers are going to do further business with you, you have to keep the quality of your budget product high. Making a low-quality product that you sell for cheap will only ensure that you never have repeat customers. People need to trust and respect you in order to do further business, so if the only transaction they ever have with you is a low value, low quality product, they aren't going to do business with you again.

Richie Rich

On the other end of the price spectrum is the luxury niche. Generally, going down the luxury route means a lot more profit. What people usually don't realize about the luxury niche is that most high-ticket items are not as affected by market conditions as budget or moderately priced items. Why? Because the rich tend to stay just that: rich. People with money tend to not skimp on their spending habits, no matter the state of the economy. Some examples of companies that target the luxury niche are: in the UK, Harrods, BA first class for flights or The Dorchester hotel; in America, hotels like Waldorf-Astoria or the Ritz Carlton. All of the big fashion labels like Armani, Gucci Versace are in the luxury category, as well as the motor vehicle companies like Rolls Royce, Cadillac and Jaguar.

When you are deciding on a price for the product or service your business will sell, do it with a specific strategy in mind. Many people just go down the budget route, most likely because it offers the lowest start-up cost, and it shoots them in the foot. I never try to be the cheapest in any product that I offer. It may sound odd, but most people think a better product is one you pay more for.

Chapter 5

Idea Generation Part Three: Packaging

The next section of the idea generation method is called **the package**. Packaging is simply the manner in which you present your product or service to the public. There are many ways of changing the packaging of existing products or services and creating your own brand. We'll look at several of them, including combining, dividing, removing, and changing the style.

The Pert Plus Revolution

The first method of packaging is what I call **combining**. It is the process of mixing several products together and selling them as something greater than the individual idea. Combining comes in a few different forms, so I will give you several different examples to explain them. The first example that comes to mind is shampoo and conditioner. Originally they were sold separately, then someone decided that having them in the same bottle would save people time in the shower and therefore be worth more than either product on its own. Sometimes combining can seem silly, but turn out to be quite profitable. Canned baked beans are an excellent example. A hundred years ago some bloke had beans and then some bright spark chose to put tomato sauce on them. I guess that's how Heinz baked beans came about.

Another method of combining is the combination of services, such as flights, hotel and car rentals. Instead of selling one at a time, companies decided to band together to a whole package of services at a special rate. This creates convenience for the customer, and helps each company promote the other.

A more ridiculous example is the beer hat. Someone decided a hat could hold your beer and funnel it directly into your mouth, freeing up the hands of sports fans. Now they can hold up their banner for their favorite football star without having to put down their beer bottle first. Hats have also been combined with radios and mp3 players, where headphones come from the hat. Another terrific example of the combining variety of packaging is what McDonald's has done with their meals. Instead of selling just a burger, I understand McDonald's makes a billion a year or so by simply asking, "Do you want that as a meal?" Originally, they asked, "Do you want fries with that?" Now they've expanded the concept even further. Bill Gates became the richest man in the world bundling software together with hardware.

Think of the health market people had been taking vitamins and drinking bottled water for decades before some bright spark put them together and got vitaminwater. The rapper 50 cent i am told walked away with $150 million from that idea. And in hindsight it's so incredibly obvious. So what else of you and I missed?

Sometimes the idea of combining can be simplified by putting one product inside another. One example is the massage chair. Back massagers have been packaged inside chair backs in order to make the self-massage possible and convenient. Some companies have made a great profit when someone realized that people like to sip coffee while reading. Now most major bookstore chains have coffee shops inside them.

As micro-technology advances, mobile phones have become the ultimate example of successfully packaging one item inside another. Initially they added an electronic calendar, then a camera, a web browser, an mp3 player, a full keyboard and now they are available as mini computers complete with a billion other apps courtesy of Steve Jobs at apple.

Long Division

The next part of packaging is what I call **dividing**. Tool kits are taken apart and sold in their component parts. Remote controlled cars and boats are sold by magazines in component parts as well. A magazine will sell you a bit of a model car or boat a time. They sell you a gear set, or wheels, or the engine piecemeal instead of all at once, which allows them to make more money.

Multi-part courses are another terrific example of dividing one product into pieces that end up costing more than the whole. Mail order correspondence courses could be easily sold as one book. By dividing the course into sections, they sell you a course ongoing over time. They've taken the materials apart, making the course both more palatable for people and allowing them to make more money off of the perceived value of getting something every month.

Another example is the Franklin Mint, a worldwide brand. They sell collections of plates, chess pieces, coins and other things. They divide the collections up and sell them one at a time. Away from the mail order industry, take a look at the automobile sections of mechanics shops, garages and auto parts stores. Companies now specialize in windows, tires, exhausts, or even testing roadworthiness. You can take a business and divide it into many bits or focus on only one area, thus making a greater profit.

Trim the Fat

The next section is what I call **removing**. Sometimes, removing undesirable aspects of a product makes it more profitable. This happens all the time in the food industry. Health-conscious people, or people on specific diets look particularly for labels that read "no preservatives," "fat free," "sugar free" or "no high fructose corn syrup." Consider unleaded petrol and paint. As scientists discovered that lead was hazardous, companies made money by advertising a lack of lead in their product. Ask yourself what kind of market can be gained by removing some aspect of a product.

Dress for Success

Probably the most apparent aspect of packaging is **the look**. One of the great success stories of the last several years is what Apple has done for electronics. Computers and music players used to all be a generic grey or black, until the introduction of the *i*Mac and its multiple colors or "flavors." Suddenly *i*Macs were the biggest selling computers, and a few years later, they succeeded again with a line of "nanochromatic" iPods.

Historically, offering a product in multiple colors has increased sales. Henry Ford originally said, "You can have any color, as long as it's black." Eventually people started wanting different colored cars so the car companies that offered a selection of colors profited. Fridges are generally white, but there is a company out there at the moment with the unfortunate name of Smeg that makes multicolored fridges to go with your interior design. Now you can accessorize your kitchen based on color.

I'm Looking Through You

Transparency can sometimes have the same effect. Some examples are skeleton watches in which you can see the inner workings of your watch, transparent car hoods to show off large engines, and again, Apple profited of off transparency by having a clear plastic cover over the iMac. Restaurants now show you the chefs cooking in the background rather than hidden away.

You *Can* Take it with You

The next innovation of packaging is called, **make it portable**. Making items more portable can be a great opportunity for coming up with some business ideas. Let's look at some of the obvious examples. Board games moved out of the home and into the car with the ingenious idea of travel games. Kids could amuse themselves on long trips by playing connect four, chess, checkers, drafts, and so on. Now they have hand-held PSPs. Phones first came off the wall with the invention of cordless phones you could carry around the house, and now we have cellular phones.

Thinking of ways to make things portable has driven all manners of profitable business. Think how portability changed the way people listen to music. In the early 1900s, you could only listen to music at home on your Victrola. The transistor radio was all the rage in the 1960s, and then during the '80s Sony invented the Walkman,   starting a whole mobile music generation now populated by various mp3 players and your mobile phone.

A slight twist on the idea of portability is food delivery. Now you can have your food brought to you or packaged in a way that makes it easy to eat on the go. The possibilities of making things portable are practically limitless. Even chairs and houses have been made portable. Think about items that are a standard part of every day life and how you could package them "to go." Almost anything you come up with could be a success.

Supersize Me

Sometimes a product can be made more profitable simply by being larger. The concept **make it bigger** can help you repackage your item in a more desirable way. Instead of having corner grocery stores we now have supermarkets and hypermarkets, which have revolutionized the way we buy food. The same thing has happened with hardware stores. They have now been combined with lumber yards to make huge home improvement centers, where even the shopping carts are over-sized. Hotels, originally small inns and bed and breakfasts have gotten bigger and bigger to the point of being entire resorts unto themselves. Perhaps you have seen the late-night TV adverts about "natural male enhancement." Those companies are taking a more unique route to profiting off of the "bigger is better" concept.

Shrinkage

On the flipside of making it bigger is **make it smaller**. Almost any electronic technology is made more profitable by being smaller. Bose took the entire home speaker system and fit it into the small, table-top Wave Radio. The original mobile phones were as big as brief cases and are now so small they can fit in your pocket. Cars get both bigger and smaller, think about SUVs and Hummers on one side, or Smart Cars and Minicoopers on the other. Both target specific markets which give them more overall success.

Pick Up the Pace

The next section is what I call **do it faster**. In the modern world, with time constraints being what they are and everyone in such a hurry, if you can find a way to save people time, you will gain a competitive advantage over your marketplace. Fast food chains are the obvious example here. Others include the "while you wait" services like photo processing, opticians and oil changes. If you can think of something that you can make quicker for people, you can find a market for it

Other examples can be found within the exercise field. Why spend the time on a full trip to the gym when you can have 8 minute Abs? Speeding up processes can apply to other aspects of your business as well. If you can provide quick, efficient customer service you can win over a clientele. Generally, think of the concept of "instant gratification." If you can fill a need or desire quicker than others, you will find yourself at an advantage in the marketplace.

The Tortoise Triumphs

Do it more slowly follows as the opposite side of the coin. Think of the car wash. Initially, this was a long drawn-out process and then someone developed a machine to automate it and make it faster. Now the washing machines are viewed as possibly damaging to the finish of your car, so more expensive car owners are reverting back to wanting their cars washed by hand: soaped, dried and polished carefully. Offering attention to detail can sometimes make your service more marketable than speed. Instead of having a 5 minute massage, you can have a full body massage over a couple of hours, or why stop there when you can spend an entire day relaxing at the health spa? If you see something that's always been done in one particular way, ask yourself, what would the effect be if I did the opposite? Often the result is an innovative profit-making idea.

She Has a Great Personality

With the **convert to a benefit** technique, you can actually repackage your flaws into desirable traits. Avis took a unique selling proposition when they were named the second largest car rental company. They converted their problem into a benefit by saying, "We're number two, so we try harder." If you can see something within the industry that looks like a complaint or problem, ask yourself how you can convert that to a benefit.

Shape Shifting

One way to change the packaging of items is to simply **change their shape**. Think about how many times styles of all sorts of things have changed. Jeans have gone through many different shapes and styles: flairs, boot cuts, skinny and drainpipe, to name a few. Just changing the shape of something may create an opportunity for you. Think about things that are every day items that have changed in shape like chairs or beds or tables or practically every other household item.

Another Place to Sell

Finally, **change the promotion**. If your product or service has always been sold one way, look at other ways to sell it. If press releases have always been used to sell your product or service, you might use other forms of advertising: direct mail, telemarketing or internet marketing (Through websites, ebay or amazon.) If the product has always been sold door-to-door, consider other methods. If you can change how a product is sold, you can often increase sales.

Seeing Green

One last piece of advice about generating ideas: **Develop your 'money goggles.'** Always keep an eye out for opportunities. Read through the idea generation section over and over again until you have all of these methods down. Walk around constantly thinking about how to apply them to products or services you see sold successfully. Remember, you can come up with a million ideas, but a million-dollar idea is not a million-dollar idea until you have successfully brought it to the marketplace.

One thing to avoid is generating only ideas without implementing them. This can be called an "idea avalanche." You get stuck and overwhelmed by the amount of opportunities and ideas you have and never move forward with any of them. Don't fall into that trap! Come up with a load of ideas and then I'll lead you on what I call "the fastest path to cash" to help you turn your ideas into successes.

The Hundred

Before sticking with one idea for your new business, you should brainstorm at least a hundred ideas. In the space below you will find one hundred lines for your one hundred ideas. In order to come up with one hundred ideas, you will need to start asking yourself some questions.

What are my customers looking for? What problems can I solve? What do people need? What are people prepared to pay for? What solutions do people really want? What information is really needed by people? You want to brainstorm at least a hundred ideas and of those hundred you are bound to get at least one or two that will work for you. You might think a hundred ideas is a lot of ideas. Not really. With the initial idea generation strategies I've given you, you should very easily be able to come up with five or ten ideas, but if you start really barreling through and constantly asking the questions above, brainstorming over and over, asking yourself constantly, what else can I think of? You will be able to do it.

Go through every area of the idea generation section, looking at all the different opportunities to develop ideas and you should easily come up with at least a hundred. If you decide to break it down just come up with ten ideas over ten days.

Bedtime with Ben

A friend of mine, Ben, once made a suggestion to me. He told me to write down these questions on a piece of paper: "What do people need? How can I add value to people's lives? How can I deliver useful products, values, or services to people?" Then he said put the paper under my pillow. The very act of writing it down and leaving it my pillow meant that I knew it was there and thought about those questions as I was going to sleep. If you try Ben's suggestion, you will find that somehow your subconscious stews and brews during the night and comes up with ideas and solutions. I have used this idea myself and found it effective. I have woken up with ideas and strategies that I don't believe I could have without using this technique.

Nobody Likes a Critic

When coming up with your hundred ideas, don't restrict yourself. Don't judge. Don't filter. Write down anything that comes to mind. The more you get away from trying to filter what you're doing, the better your ideas will become. Once you start getting into the idea generation process, some good ideas will come at the start, some further on, but as you get closer to idea 100, you will start to come up with some unbelievably great ideas that wouldn't seem obvious to you at the start. So I do urge you to write down a hundred ideas.

Once you have the hundred ideas down, and only once they are all on paper, start to filter through them. Concentrate on maybe the ten or twelve best ideas you find. Once you've got the ten or twelve best ideas, later on I will give you some questions you can ask of each of them. After this course, you will be able to find the one or two that will make the most sense and give you a direct path to developing the business idea you want. With a hundred ideas you get an awful lot of flexibility. You may take yourself down a successful path you wouldn't have thought of had you stopped after the first four or five. In the fantastic book "Choose Yourself" by James Altucher he suggests as part of his daily routine coming up with 10 new ideas a day. I know it sounds daunting but ones you start to exercise your idea muscle it will begin to become much easier. Give it a go.

Quick tip. Once you have your ideas. You might like to brainstorm ten ideas on how you would start to get that business of the ground.
This gives you the first steps of execution which in the final analyses is what will get your business of the ground.

Have at it.

1.

_____

_____

2.

_____

_____

3.

_____

_____

4.

_____

_____

5.

_____

_____

6.

_____

___

7.

_____

___

8.

_____

___

9.

_____

___

10.

_____

___

11.

_____

___

12.

_____

___

13.

_____

___

14.

_____

___

15.

___

16.

___

17.

___

18.

___

19.

___

20.

___

21.

___

22.

___

23.

_____

_____

24.

_____

_____

25.

_____

_____

26.

_____

_____

27.

_____

_____

28.

_____

_____

29.

_____

_____

30.

_____

_____

31.

_____

_____

32.

_____

___

33.

_____

___

34.

_____

___

35.

_____

___

36.

_____

___

37.

_____

___

38.

_____

___

39.

_____

___

40.

___

41.

___

42.

___

43.

___

44.

___

45.

___

46.

___

47.

___

48.

___

49.

___

50.

___

51.

___

52.

___

53.

___

54.

___

55.

___

56.

___

57.

___

58.

___

59.

___

60.

___

61.

___

62.

___

63.

___

64.

___

65.

___

66.

___

67.

___

68.

___

69.

___

70.

___

71.

___

72.

___

73.

___

74.

_____

___

75.

_____

___

76.

_____

___

77.

_____

___

78.

_____

___

79.

_____

___

80.

_____

___

81.

_____

___

82.

_____

___

83.

_____

___

84.

_____

___

85.

_____

___

86.

_____

___

87.

_____

___

88.

_____

___

89.

_____

___

90.

_____

___

91.

_____

__

92.

_____

__

93.

_____

__

94.

_____

__

95.

_____

__

96.

_____

__

97.

_____

__

98.

_____

__

99.

_____

__

Chapter 6

Obtaining Resources

Every entrepreneur needs to obtain resources-- finance, knowledge and skills—to begin their business. The most common approach that most people new to entrepreneurial ventures take is using their own skills and their own finances. This can turn out to be a regrettable method.

Anything You Can Do I Can Do Better

The mistake I made for many a long year that held me back more than anything else is the "I can do it better than anyone else" mentality. It is the feeling that the only person who can do things and sort everything out is you. If you are very left-brained or logical like I am, you may tend to think that other people don't think the same way as you or act the same as you or put the same effort in as you do. Every early entrepreneurial endeavor I made, of which there are many, some successful, some not so successful, I financed myself. I fronted the money for all of them. I never accepted any loans. All the money that I had worked for and saved, I used to get my endeavors going and growing.

In addition to obtaining finances, an entrepreneur needs skills. There are a lot of skills you need when developing your entrepreneurial endeavors. To successfully begin your business, you will need knowledge of your marketplace; you will need to know how to generate ideas; you will need salesmanship skills, marketing skills, and maybe also technical skills, technology skills maybe even things you don't yet know you need to know. There are many skills and a good amount of knowledge you will need, and too many people try to bring them all to the table themselves.

I'm not saying that using all your own personal knowledge, skills and finances is an impossible route to take. In fact, many people have done it that way. All I'm saying is that if you want to get a really successful entrepreneurial endeavor going, it's not the best way. It's one way. You definitely don't want to go down that route if you can help it. For some people, it's the only route available. And if that's the route you have to go down, take it one step at a time, and do your best. But there is a better way.

Other People's Experience

As we discussed, many people looking for resources tend to go down the route of using their own skills, their own money and their own knowledge. In this section I will tell you about Other People's Resources. Other people's resources come in various forms, and I'll start with the one that I think is the most important: other people's experience.

Experience is the single best resource for getting you to where you want to go in the business world. You don't have to have your own, necessarily. There are effective ways to get experience from other people. A strategy I've used in practically every endeavor I've ever undertaken is called picking brains.

Follow the Leader

To pick someone's brain is to obtain the knowledge of another person who has, and this is the important part, *walked the path that you want to walk before you've walked it.* There are an awful lot of budding businessmen who go and ask advice from those who have never walked the path they want to walk. For example, many a person discusses their attempted business endeavor with friends down at the pub, family members and work colleagues. They ask these people for their knowledge and skills and ideas. They ask their opinions. More often than not, these random people are not in an entrepreneurial mindset, and they will advise against the endeavor.

These are not the people you want to ask for advice about your business. They will hold you back. They think they are looking out for you, so they will tell you not to try something. Most people will settle for mediocrity, or the status quo. Most people, when you talk about taking a risk, will try and stop you from taking that risk, basically because they don't want to look bad. So when picking brains, you want to go to people who have already done what you want to do.

Beep Beep

Let's say you are in the car parts business. What you should do is look in the yellow pages or on the Internet and find someone who is already in the industry, who already has a business that is successful, and who is in a non-competitive or a non-geographically close location. Contact this person by letter, email or phone, and say "Hello, I understand you are in this business. I'm just starting out in this same business and I'm wondering if you could spare five minutes of your time to help me avoid any mistakes I might be likely to make."

You might be surprised how many people will actually say "Yes" to this request. Most business owners, if they've been in the business for a reasonable period of time and are successful, never get to speak to anyone about it. Their spouses don't want to hear about it anymore and their friends might not be as successful and don't want to hear about it.

Another reason they might want to tell you about their career is simple modesty no one normally likes to brag so they always keep their story to themselves. They have no outlet to get their story heard. Many people don't like to blow their own trumpets, as it were, because it seems like bad form. Perhaps this is truer here in Great Britain than it is in America, because there it seems business success is viewed as part of the 'American Way.' Discussing these successes is a more of a noble pursuit there than it is in staid and stilted Great Britain. Nevertheless, you will definitely find people willing to talk to you.

Twenty Questions

When you get to speak to someone in your industry who is willing to discuss their experiences, you should have a list of questions ready. Your first question should be: How did you get started in your business? Ask them about their biggest successes. Ask them to tell you the stories of their triumphs, all the best things that ever happened to them, all the great learning experiences they had, and all the shortcuts they discovered over time.

On the flip side of that, you want to ask them about their failures. What could they have avoided but didn't? What knowledge didn't they have that would have moved them further? What would they have wanted to know at the start that they now know and would have made their journey into the business that much easier?

The most important question you can ask someone whose brains you are picking is *how* they run their business. What processes do they use in every area of their business? How did they find their first customers? How did they close their first sale? Ask them about any processes that go along with the business, such as sales, marketing, production, inventory, or processes in supplying and manufacturing. Any processes you think might be appropriate for your business you need to glean from the people who have been there.

Once you have finished talking to that person, don't stop there. You want to pick the brains of as many people you can get on the phone. Each person you ask may know 90% of all there is to know within their industry, so by asking several people your questions, you increase the range of information you will get. If you go and talk to 10 or 15 people, you can actually gain more knowledge in a few days/weeks than it took them ten years to learn. It may seem unnecessary to do this, but you will glean a more valuable education about the business you want to start than you would at any university especially the university of trial and error. The knowledge of their experience will speed you down the road to your own successful business.

Show Me the Way

The next way to get other people's experience is through mentors. A mentor is a business person who has already seen their fair amount of success and is ready to impart his/her wisdom to you. A lot of people who have retired as a success feel like they are not offering value anymore. If you can come along and give them the opportunity to give value, they will appreciate you for it.

When looking for mentors, you need to find people who can remain in close contact with you, and often this means they need to live nearby. There are several ways to find a mentor. You could speak to a retired businessman in your community whom you like or respect. Maybe someone you know who has been successful, a friend of the family, a family member or someone you know from the local news would be willing to help you. Maybe you ask other business people who was great in the business who has recently left the business. Don't be afraid to contact these people. I'm not guaranteeing that they are going to say yes, but more often than not, they will. People who have left the business world still have all their knowledge and skills are often happy to pass their experience on to the next generation.

With all the possibilities out there, you want to make sure to choose your mentor wisely. Too many people get the mentor-mentee relationship wrong. There are a few aspects of your relationship with your mentor that you need to ensure. First of all, you have to actually like the person. If you find a mentor who has all the knowledge and skills that you really want, but you don't actually like them, then I'll be honest with you, you aren't going to listen to that person. You're not going to trust their advice and you're not going to respect it. And you may battle with them when there's no good reason to battle.

The second part of your relationship with a mentor is trust. If you don't trust the people you choose as mentors, then they're not going to really be positive mentors at all. You have to know that the advice they give you is in your best interest, and that they are saying it with your best interests in mind. You have to trust the person that you are taking on as a mentor.

You have to respect your mentor. If you find a mentor who's not exactly what you want, or you realize that they were untruthful or practiced business in a way that you don't like, you won't respect them. The relationship has to be based on trust and respect, so if you don't respect that person, the relationship will turn sour sooner or later.

You also want commonality. You want to find a common ground with this person. I met one of my earliest mentors at my golf course. We could walk around the golf course discussing my business situations and issues that I had, and he was more than happy to pass on his information. We had golf as a commonality, but you could have anything in common with your mentor: a love of chess, poker, books, food, films or sport. I wouldn't suggest a beer buddy as the best choice for a mentor, but who knows, it may be. Look for someone who has some sort of commonality with you, and that will make the relationship far more enjoyable and beneficial.

One final point, if there are successful people in the sector you want to go into, see if they have a business biography/book. In the past, I have used biographies/books of people to try to get an understanding of their thinking process and their methodologies. This practice of benefitting from fictitious mentors leads me to the next topic: masterminding.

Chapter 7

The Mastermind Group

The mastermind theory was originally presented by Napoleon Hill in his classic book *Think and Grow Rich*, commissioned by Andrew Carnegie. In the section called masterminding, Hill discusses two varieties, the normal and the internal.

A mastermind group is a group of people who are like-minded and are all looking to succeed. For example, if you're looking to start a business and you find a few other people who are also looking to start a business, either with you or on their own, you will have some commonality and share some problems. You want to choose at least some people who are specifically outside your business so that you can obtain perspective from other people's knowledge in other industries. Sometimes they will offer you advice that is common in their industry, but may be very dynamic within your sector.

A mastermind group consists of at least two, but preferably six to eight people. I wouldn't suggest more than eight, which would be too large. You all have to be equally motivated, and each must be equally personally honest and have integrity. The format of a mastermind group is that you will meet at a specific time and date at certain time intervals. Some people get together once a week, or once a month, some once a fortnight. I wouldn't suggest any longer a time interval than once a month; I would think that would be the bare minimum. The more often you meet, the faster you will accelerate your process.

The structure of a mastermind group involves sitting down and discussing your problems with each other. First go over what happened the last time you met and the problems that you had previously. Then discuss individually each problem that you are facing. Once you lay out these problems, the other people within your mastermind group will offer up ideas and solutions and strategies to help you solve the issues that you face. Sometimes you will not be facing any issues, and they will just be there for general encouragement, as you will be there to encourage and help those who actually are facing problems at that moment.

On the flip side when no problems are happening you can ask for ideas of rapid improvement and see what people can come up with.

The mastermind group is an incredible resource. You will find that sometimes problems absolutely stump you simply because you are too close to the problem to see a solution. These issues can be solved by the group, who will be able to come up with ideas and solutions that can quickly and efficiently help you get past the problems that you are facing. And who knows they may just come up with a blockbuster idea that hits your business out of the park. If meeting with a group of real people isn't an option for you, there is an alternative.

Voices in Your Head

There is a second method of masterminding that is contained in Hill's book. At one stage I was concerned about discussing that idea, called the internal mastermind group, but now I am comfortable with my own 'insanity'. In the book, he talks about having an inner boardroom, where he met with various imaginary advisors. He imagined them sitting around a large table. He would ask questions and they would give him answers. Obviously, to most anyone who hasn't tried this, it sounds insane. The idea of creating a mastermind group of people from fantasy or history is a bit mental.

Before you judge, I'll tell you a bit about my experiences with this method. Originally when I tried this idea, these are the people I imagined in my boardroom: Leonardo Da Vinci, Sir James Goldsmith, a few literary characters who I admired, such as Don Vito Corleone, and a few weird people like Hannibal Lecter, Warren Buffett and even Anthony Robbins.

This is how it worked. I would imagine a room. In the room was a table, I was at the head of the table which had four seats on either side, and two seats at the end. The two at the end were what I called guest seats, meant for special advisors. Of occasion I would imagine people not on my regular board who could solve specific problems, bring them in and ask them questions. One of the people I had sitting at the end of my table at one stage was Paul Atreides from Frank Herbert's book *Dune*. He was able to see the future, which I thought was a useful skill. He could help me solve problems before they actually happened.

Over the years I read various business biographies, and biographies of other people I respected. Once I had an idea of who those people were and what their personality type was, they were likely to get an invitation to my boardroom.

Other invitations went out to characters from TV programs, books and movies (like I said, I took one from *The Godfather*). In the '90s there was a program in the UK called *Chancer* and I had the lead character Stephen Crane, a business analyst who took a lot of chances, on my board.

Choose Your Imaginary Friends Wisely

I should explain why I included Hannibal Lecter, along with some other weird characters, like Keyser Söze from the film *The Usual Suspects*. Basically, each character had some trait that I thought was useful to get me where I wanted to go. Each had something I needed, or at least thought I needed at the time.

Keyser Söze had absolute will. If you've ever seen the film, then you'll understand that characteristic. Don Vito Corleone was quite the businessman generally, and also had a way of motivating people and securing their loyalty. Hannibal Lecter, apart from the small foible he had of gruesomely killing people, had great taste and style. He was elegant and full of class. Leonardo Da Vinci was obviously brought in for his absolute genius and creativity. Anthony Robbins used to make appearances when things weren't necessarily going my way. I would bring him in for some extra motivation.

To have a board meeting, I'd go into my boardroom, or my head. I'd sit down at the table, greet all of my guests, and introduce new people that day if there were any. I would tell them all the reason that we were convening. I would tell them the problems I was facing. I would also thank them for being honest and open with me and let them know that anything they said would not be offensive to me, and I would take it all to heart.

Again, I understand this sounds mildly insane. I'm sure the many a psychiatrist would commit me for my admission of this practice. Yet, if you are honest with yourself, you will admit that you have weaknesses. Be particularly introspective and identify these weaknesses. When confronted by a problem that either exposes or is due to these weaknesses, imagining a person that you know or have read about who has strengths in these areas will often allow you to see your way out of your problem.

Anyway, I'd go ask questions of these people who were, as I was well aware, in my head. I'd ask them questions about the problems I was facing and say, "What do you think of this?" and "what do you think of that?" I'd go around the table and ask them individually. As weird as this will sound, I got answers from my internal mastermind group that I don't believe came from myself. Yes, I know, that sounds daft. I would ask questions and answers would come from these people. Maybe it was just because I was allowing myself and my ego to get out of the way, but I don't know the psychological tenets of why that would work. I have no clue. I know it worked for Napolean Hill, and that's why I tried it. I was skeptical at first, but I found it did work. And it's worked for me ever since.

Over time I have occasionally forgotten about my internal set of advisors, but every time I have faced a major challenge, I've gone back to my boardroom. Depending on the period in my life, there have been various changes to my boardroom members. Usually I imagined those that had characteristics I was weak on at the time. And I got answers to questions from these characters.

The members of your boardroom could be real or fictional, historical or alive and well today. Some present-day members I could see as being of some use are Bill Gates, Richard Branson, Oprah Winfrey, Donald Trump or Steve Jobs. If you wanted to go further back in history you might want Thomas Edison or John D. Rockefeller in your boardroom, maybe Andrew Carnegie or Alexander the Great.

I apologize to some of you for this section, because I know it sounds absolutely mad. But for those of you who are brave enough and actually have the courage to try and experiment with the internal mastermind group, I genuinely believe you will have a *tangible* advantage over those who do not try it. If you read a lot of biographies, which I encourage you to do, about successful people you want to model your ideas after, your boardroom will be occupied by the kind of successful people who can help you solve problems.

Even if you are not inviting these successful people to your internal boardroom, you can still model your practices after them. Modeling is another of the strategies you can employ to gain other people's knowledge. You can model people's skills, strategies and styles. Perhaps you should read a couple of Bill Gates's biographies to get a feeling for who the man is, and how he does business. You will then be able to either model your business approach after him or include him in your internal mastermind group, where, surprisingly I know, you could get many of the ideas and strategies that he would have.

So I encourage you to use both types of masterminding, both internal and external, and the practice of modeling. If you don't feel brave enough to attempt the internal mastermind group, then developing a physical mastermind group of actual people is a must.

Chapter 8

Other People's Ideas

The next section on other people's resources is other people's ideas. I told you in an idea generation section earlier that one of the ideal ways to develop ideas is to model someone else's. The reason I said to model other people's ideas is because they are proven; you can use their blueprint. If you are one of the people who struggles to develop ideas, then I see there being nothing wrong in looking around for successful business models that are working and adopting their ideas. Modeling other people's ideas is generally a good practice because their ideas are proven strategies that clearly work and are successful.

Stealing Isn't Always Wrong

The second method of using other people's ideas may sound horrible, though in reality I find it morally acceptable. It is to steal other people's ideas. Modeling, you could say, is a form of stealing although it's described in much nicer language. Sir Isaac Newton said, "If I have been able to see further than others, it is because I have stood on the shoulders of giants." Much of human progress is based on modeling and stealing ideas.

Let's say you're sitting down at the pub and you're with some mates and one of your mates comes up with an idea that is fantastic. In fact, it may be the next great business idea, but you know in your heart of hearts that your mate will never actually do anything with that idea. Eventually someone will do something with that idea when they spontaneously create it on their own. Well, I see it as morally acceptable to take that idea and run with it if you know the person with the idea is never going to do anything with it. I don't see why you shouldn't actually put it to use.

If you want to be a little more scrupulous, why not partner up with your mate? If they've come up with the idea and you have all the motivation and dynamism to actually get that idea off the ground, going and growing then you have the basis for a viable partnership. You can use the information that you've gained in this course to do so. If it makes you feel more comfortable, partner up with these inactive idea generators.

If you want to go it alone and know that all they were good for was the idea, then your next action depends on your moral stance. I'd be quite comfortable if you and I took that idea and ran with it, adopting it as our own. If you can make a successful business out of that idea, then there's nothing stopping you from providing the person whose idea it originally was with some fiscal remuneration . . . and a bit of a "thank you."

Either way, the choice is yours, but as I say, modeling and stealing are business ideas that are employed every single day in the real world to great effect. It happens far more often than you would presume (just look at some of the lawsuits going on in the tech world over intellectual property rights), so I wouldn't get into any moral dilemmas or qualms about adopting the strategy of stealing ideas, because it is a standard business practice in every area of the world.

Note: Ok so if the idea works the person who came up with the idea may want to take you to court to get "their fair share", but don't let that stop you. It didn't stop Mark Zuckerberg and he got sued by the Winklevos twins. For reportedly $60 million!!! Sounds like a big ouch until you realise that Zuck is worth well over $20 billion. So not so bad after all.

These are two of the great ways of getting a successful business started quickly. They are especially useful when modeling an existing business in a different location and using the lag time process that I discuss in the idea generation section.

Chapter 9

Other People's Money

I'm going to give you a quick summary of the four keys to being a successful candidate for someone else's money. You need to read and understand these before I proceed talking about Other People's Money.

Money lenders are looking for four major things when considering new investments.

1. They need to be predisposed to lending you money.
2. They are usually looking for a return, hopefully a high return.
3. They are looking for little or no risk.
4. They want to have some degree of control in their own hands.

As I talk about the following money-lending institutions and groups of people, bear these four points in mind.

Take it to the Bank

The second place after their own money that most people go to get money is a bank. Usually, people start with their own bank. Your bank may or may not lend you money depending both upon your credit rating and what sort of a relationship you have with the bank. It is possible that your bank might simply not be predisposed to lending money to a business venture in your sector. If this is the case, then you have two options. You could either think about starting a different business in a sector more favored by your bank, or look to another lending institution that is predisposed to lending money to ventures within the sector of your choice.

There are lending institutions that have predispositions towards a variety of industries or business sectors. You need to research sectors and find out who the main bankers are for each one. Once you choose an area, you can specify your search for money.

Let's say that you're in the furniture manufacturing business. You should find out who usually deals with that sector because they will have knowledge of furniture manufacturing, how it works and what it will take to get your business growing. From a lending institution's perspective, lending money to businesses in sectors they are both familiar with and have experience in will allow them to have some control. They also know the risks involved in that sector. Because they know those things going in, they will be more predisposed to make a loan in that area. When you are looking for banks, look for the ones that are predisposed to loan *to your sector*. Hey, they may even be able to give you great advice and show you some shortcuts or even introduce you to people who they think will help you through their pre-existing network.

Another strategy to find banks that will be most willing to lend you money is to find new banks. Banks that are just starting out usually have an awful lot of money to loan, and they want to make loans because that's the predominant way that banks make money. So look out for new banks opening and contact them, because they will have a much higher degree of need to lend money than a bank that's been around for twenty or thirty years. Even the bigger banks operate under the same policies; they are looking to make loans.

Another obvious sign of a bank that particularly wants to make loans is advertising. If you see a bank advertising in your local newspaper, national newspapers, or online, you know it is looking to lend money. For example, in the UK we have a site called moneysupermarket.com, and you can go there and compare the rates of different banks. If you look at all the business rates and you see one company that's specifically advertising cheap rates within your sector, then you know they've got a block of money they want to unload. That bank will be far more likely to lend you money because it has money. When banks are looking to make a return on their loans, they want to get that return as quickly as possible (It actually costs them money to hold on to if for too long). So if you do see banks that are advertising their money for borrowing, go after that opportunity. Use that money to get started. So like I said keep on the lookout for advertising.

When You've Got the Golden Seed to a Money Tree

Another way of getting money on a short-term basis if you have an idea that you think can really win is to use that same strategy for credit cards. I don't condone starting businesses with credit cards if you can get the money elsewhere, because to be quite honest, the interest you pay on credit card loans is far higher than with virtually any other method of obtaining finance. But if you've got a *sure-fire winner* that you know you can get going and growing really quickly, and *you have no other method* of obtaining finance, look for credit card companies that are advertising.

You'll usually see them in three or four sectors across the board. If they are advertised, you know they have a predisposition for lending you money.

Another option many people don't know they have is increasing their current line of credit. If you have a credit limit on existing credit cards, phone your credit card company a couple of times. Ask, "Can you increase my limits?" and they will say "by how much?" and then you say, "Well, how much are you prepared to increase my limit by?" If you do that two or three times, you will likely talk to people of different lending authority levels. You can get an awful lot of money from your credit cards simply by asking the right questions of your existing credit card companies.

As I've said, I am not condoning the use of credit cards to finance a business *unless* you have a sure-fire winner.

There are also ways of using credit cards with literally no interest. If you use one credit card and then swap that balance to another one that is offering a zero percent interest rate on bank transfers, you may be able to get an interest-free loan for a limited period of time. Again, I don't condone trying to use credit cards as a first recourse to finance your business, but as a last resort they're always an option.

If at First You Don't Succeed...

When asking for loans from banks, don't just stop after the first one you go to. On one of the first deals I ever did I was looking to buy some property. I went to *ten different banks* before one actually agreed to the deal. Most people give up after their first try because they try their own bank, ask them for a loan, are rejected and so feel dejected. Done with. I'll talk a bit later about both why people fail at business and your expectations for failure. When you are going to the bank, expect to fail. Expect them to say no and just barrel on through and keep asking banks until one of them says yes, and eventually one of them will.

So like I say, look for new banks. Look for banks that are advertising, but try them all. Start with the ones that are predisposed to lending you money, and then just barrel your way through the ones that have the potential to lend you money.

When you are going to ask someone for finance, you need to have a plan ready. You need to have as much information as you can possibly give your prospective lending institution as to why you are going to need the money. They want to know what the purpose of the money is, when you expect to be able to pay it back, and what sort of rate of return they will get. Have a business plan. Do as many smart things as you can in order to make yourself look better. Have pre-existing orders already available. Show that people have already responded to your offer. Show them that you know where your market is, you know how to reach your market and you know how much it's going to cost to reach your market. Have all these things in place when you go to ask for a loan.

When you go to a lending institution, you want to be able to say "This is what I need the money for. This is what it's going to cost. This is when I will be able to get the money back. This is when I'll be able to return it to you." The lending institutions risk evaluators will know that you are eliminating the risk for them. As I mentioned earlier, when you can offer practically no risk to the people who are looking to lend you money, they are far more likely to lend it to you.

Add Venture Capital

The next way of raising finance is venture capital. If you have a business that you really believe is going to go and grow and don't mind giving up a big percentage of the profits to the venture capitalists, then this is an option for you. I am not a huge fan of venture capitalism for the entrepreneur because you have to give up a large percent of the company, often more than you want to give up, to your venture capitalist. If you have no other way of getting finance, then maybe a venture capital firm is the way to go. There are however some major upsides in the form of skills, connections, relationships/networks, that they may come with. Some of these are worth far more than you may give up 50% of something awesome is often better than 100% of something mediocre.

Venture capital firms will need to know exactly what you expect from the business. They will need to have you answer all the big questions about your potential profits. They will need you to show that there will be a return and what sort of return they are likely to make. More than anything else, they will need to know when they are going to get their money back. If you are going to go to a venture capitalist, you need to be able show how there is an exit strategy for them.

Venture Capital firms are fairly easy to find in the yellow pages, on the Internet, or advertised locally. Venture Capital is not the ideal route that I would take to raise finance unless they come with a bucket load of connections and skills, but if you do, then go in with your eyes wide open. Realize that you are going to have to give away a large proportion of the value of your company in order to get their money.

Please, Sir, I Want Some More

Advertising for money is also a viable option to finance your business. If you believe that you have a business opportunity that will give someone a fantastic return, there's no harm in putting an advert in the newspaper. Ted Nicholas, in his book *Magic Words that Bring you Riches,* came up with a strategy for attracting business investors. According to Nicholas, you should include the words "sophisticated investor" in the headline of your advertisement. Everyone *thinks* they're a sophisticated investor because no one wants to see themself as being unsophisticated. Your advert should look something like this, "Looking for a sophisticated investor—local businessman with a great track record is looking for money to start a new business. There is a start-up opportunity with a low investment and a high potential return."

While it's not the first and foremost idea that I would try, advertising can work. In addition to printed ads, you could also hand out proposals at your local chamber of commerce meeting to attract an investor. As you would for a bank loan officer, you will need to have to have your business plan ready to show your potential investor when they inquire. You could also ask your accountant or solicitor if they know of anyone who has recently come into some money and are looking for some business opportunities. You will be surprised how many of them know someone.

A Little Help Here

The next method of obtaining finances is the most useful of them all. Usually when you start a business you have a limited amount of skills. Maybe you are a creative person. Maybe you are a great salesperson. Perhaps you are a great idea generation person. Regardless of your strengths, you will have weaknesses in other areas. One of the great ways of raising finances is getting partners. It's especially beneficial, because you might not just be getting money from them, you might also be getting something useful for your business as well. Partnership is definitely for many a way forward especially if you have skill/knowledge deficits in a particular area. The first rule of partnering is just like getting a mentor. You have to like, trust and respect them first and foremost. Second, as I have mentioned find people who have complementary skills that you lack. Finally, spend as much time as you can before you start the business so as to get a feel for them. If there is any hint that you may clash then go find someone else.

Silence is Golden

There are two types of partners that you can have. The first of these is the silent partner. You go to them and say, "Ok, this is what you get. You get to buy a piece of the business and this is the potential return you make, but you don't get any say in the general day-to-day running of the business. You don't get any input into the business. You just get a return if and when there is one." Then you show them everything you would show a bank so that they see the investment necessary, the risks involved, and have an idea of the potential profit.

Rather than discussing terms of partnership with you, your new silent partner may simply say, "Go to it." That sometimes happens. I will say this, if they do say that they want to be silent, make sure they stick to that. An awful lot of silent partners will at one stage ask to be kept regularly up-to-date about what's going on. You should dictate the terms of how that's going to work right at the outset. Don't leave it until later. Make it clear that you will be reporting to them only when you are meant to be. They won't have reports every day, unless you want them to. You have to dictate the terms upfront. If you try to work them out further on down the line, you will generally have problems.

The second type of partner is the active partner. Usually when you have an active partner, as with mentors, you need to like, trust and respect that person. The last thing you want is partner who, shortly after you get into business you decide you really don't like, you don't get on and you want them to get out. You need to find partners you like, who *add* something that you don't have to the business. There's no point in both of you being great sales people if you're also both rubbish in other areas. If you are going to get an active partner, look for someone with skill sets slightly different from yours. Partners with complementary skill sets are most effective.

Be honest with yourself and acknowledge, "This is an area where I'm actually no good." By choosing partners with regard to their skill sets in your weak areas you will cover more ground and actually help yourself in the long run.

When you are choosing people who might be potential partners, obviously you have to make sure that they have money. You have to express the percent of the business that they are going to get, what they get for that and when they're going to get it. If you're going into an industry where you know someone who already has knowledge or skill in that industry, talk to them. Let them know you are starting a business. If you find someone who is already in that area and who is ready to partially finance themselves in that business, then use that person rather than someone who has no knowledge or skills within that industry. That will take a lot of the pressure and weight off of you later.

With a Little Help from my Friends

One place where many people go for money is either a great idea or a horrific idea depending on several factors. This is sometimes one of the first places people go. They go to friends and family. Friends and family can be a great source for obtaining money, but as I've mentioned before, you need to clearly define the outcome. Define the parameters of their investment according to the four keys discussed at the beginning of this chapter.

When dealing with friends and family, integrity plays a big part. Do they believe you? Do they see you as someone who's going somewhere? Do they have faith in your capabilities? Because if they don't, they're not going to lend you the money in the first place, or if they do lend the money out of a sense of obligation, then they are constantly going to be on your back. So, again, more than in any other lending relationship, if you are going to borrow money from friends or family, you really have to clearly define and anticipate the relationship.

If you use friends and family's money, it's not like using money from banks or institutional-type investing. The weird thing is this- if you start a business with friends or family's money and that business fails to get where you want it to and the money gets lost, should you later start *another* business venture that succeeds, these people will expect to get their money back. You have to really be clear with them.

You can either say, "look, I'll borrow this money and if this business works you will obviously be paid handsomely. If it doesn't work, no matter what I will pay you back from another business endeavor eventually. This is just being borrowed from you, but whether it works or it doesn't work, you'll get your money back one way or another. Integrity with friends and family is always important. If they believe you are really serious when you say no matter what's going to happen you will always get your money back, even if the first or second venture fails, there is the potential to go back to them. Using friends and family's money can be a terrific idea, as long as you explicitly define the terms of the loan. As long as you show integrity to them, there's the potential to always go back for more.

Help from Above

The next place to get money is from business angels. Business angels are similar to venture capital firms. They will lend you money for whatever reason you need it. They expect a return on their investment. There are plenty of business angel networks all across the world, so look them up online. Business angels will do various things for you. Try to clearly define what they'll do for you, understanding that, as with venture capitalists, it will vary depending on which angels you're working with. So look them up and see what they're likely to do for you.

Granting Wishes

The next area of finance is grants. As far as I'm aware, most governments around the world offer grants for business start-ups. In the UK we have things like the Prince's Trust for small businesses. In Wales where I live, we had an organisation called the Welsh Development Agency that would give money to people who could potentially create new jobs in Wales. Local government grants tend to especially support young people, but they lend money to all sorts of people to fulfill their business goals.

Finding a grant programs is easy, so you really have no excuse not to look. Just check online or ask your local governmental bodies or citizens' advice bureaus where you are likely to find a grant in your area. Ask your local chamber of commerce people what grants are available for your sort of business. Ask within your business sector what grants are available. Just hammer out the research, because grants can be a great way of obtaining finance, and in some cases you can get that money without interest and without having to pay it back. So sometimes you literally get *free money*. In other cases you do have to pay it back, but usually under fantastically good terms. Generally, the grant programs expect you to put up some percentage of the money first, primarily to demonstrate your commitment to your business. So look into grants. They are a great way of obtaining the amount of money you need.

Safety In Numbers

One method that is starting to become immensely popular as we speak is crowd funding. I have never used this method so I am not really able to give any great insight, but I feel I would be remise in neglecting this as an option. So maybe this could be something that you should look at. Just google crowd funding and you will probably get all the information you will need.

Don't Forget Your Keys

Now you have the methods of obtaining finance; venture capital, partners, friends and family, business angels, and grants. Knowing who to go to for finance is one thing, but without knowing how to convince them to give you money, that knowledge won't be of much help. As I mentioned at the start of this chapter, there are four keys to obtaining all the money you will ever want.

The first of these keys is the predisposition of the lender to do business with you. If you can find someone who is in the habit of lending money to people just like you, then go to them first. Sometimes that person is a family member who you know would do anything for you, a clear demonstration of predisposition. When choosing an institutional lender, make sure you are going to a lender that is predisposed to your industry. If your business requires assets and you discover that there is a specific asset-based lender, go to them.

Un-risky Business

The second key is your ability to show the lenders that through your business they will get not only their money back, but a good return on their investment. Depending on which lender you choose, they will expect more or less of a return. Venture capitalists will probably expect the greatest return, and banks less. Partners, friends and family members will probably expect some return, but it is possible that some family members or friends won't even expect a return at all. In this case, I suggest you offer them something, because it will give them a greater incentive to lend you money in the future. Always look to how you can offer people the highest potential return.

The third key to obtaining money is eliminating risk. The best way to do that is by doing all your research before meeting with a potential investor. That research involves most of the items I have covered so far throughout this course. Make sure that you have found your market, found out how big it is and what the market wants, developed your idea and made sure that your future customers are prepared to pay for your product. With that information, you can extrapolate how much money your business is going to be able to make, or at least the potential money you can make from the marketplace.

If you can show that your business has a fantastically high rate of potential success, then you are eliminating an awful lot of risk for the people who will be financing you. You can show your would-be investors that you are a worthwhile candidate for receiving their money. You usually won't be able to eliminate all the risk, but it is possible. Sometimes you will have already received money for your product before you even go to ask for the loan. When you are able to demonstrate that people are already so enthusiastic about the business or product that you're about to develop that they have begun to pay you for it, a lender would be irresponsible *not* to fund you. Your main goal should be to limit your risk as much as possible.

Control Freak

The final key to getting other people's resources is putting at least some of the control in their hands. Keep in mind that you must be clear about the extent of your investors' control. Control can mean giving them a percentage of the business, being accountable to them, or if it's from a partner's perspective, letting them know that they will have a certain amount of involvement in the business.

If you have advisors from your venture capital firm or business angels who have knowledge or experience within your market and can give you advice, their involvement can actually be helpful to you. With some of the control in their hands, they will be far more favorable to your requests than if they had no control. At the end of the day, they are lending you their money, and they want to have some amount of influence over what's done with that money.

You know who to ask for the money your new business needs, and how to convince them to give it to you. You now have the tools to successfully obtain other people's resources.

Chapter 10

Other People's Time and Work

Time. We all have a limited amount of it. There are only 24 hours in the day, and no matter what we do, we can't bargain with life to give us more any more time in a day. Whether you are a billionaire or a pauper on the street, you are all restricted to 24 hours in a day. That being said, some people's time is more valuable than others. Depending on how you are running your business, you will know there will be certain actions that earn you more money than others. I call these *forward essence actions*. These are the actions that will get you to where you want to go and earn you more money. These are the actions that you want to concentrate on.

Do the Math

Before you know which actions are going to earn you the most money, you need to learn how to value your time. Time has a certain price per minute. You should ask yourself the question, "How much do I want to actually earn from my business?" Once you have that figure on a piece of paper, you want to divide that by 52 for the weeks in the year, and then divide that number by 40 hours. We'll call 40 hours a five-times-eight working week. Once you've got the hourly rate you want to earn, I would suggest you multiply that by 4. Because of the 8 hours a day you are likely to work in a standard work week, usually you will only get 2 really productive hours. Whatever you think your hourly rate is in a day, multiply that hourly rate by 4. In reality, the likelihood that you will get 8 hours of productive work time in your day is just non-existent. Now you can value your time and know what it is worth.

Look at the above figure as the cost of your time and then look at the actions that don't earn you, or don't have the potential of earning you that amount of money for the time spent. Once you have that time amount allocated, you can go about buying time more cheaply. If at the start of your business you can't afford to buy time more cheaply, you know then that the first thing you have to do, out of all the tasks you have to complete in your day, is look at the tasks that have the potential of earning the sort of money you want.

Divide your tasks by time value or the potential of time value, and do them in order of the ones that get you closer to your time value. They are the tasks to concentrate on. An awful lot of the time, most people in business will do the tasks or the actions that do *not* have the potential of earning them the most money. When you can value your time and the time in your day and denominate the time in an amount, you will know which tasks to get on with.

Most people in business spend too much time on the actions that don't earn them any money. I'm giving you a way of actually understanding time and the management of your time based on fiscal remuneration, or getting the money in.

Once you have valued your time and you can afford to pay people for less, evaluate the tasks to be accomplished. Rank the tasks by value and whether or not they can be delegated. Take the most forward essence actions that can be delegated and find workers to do them for far less than your own time is worth.

Buying Other People's Time, or

Because You're Too Good for a Sweatshop

Obviously the usual route is just employing staff. You want to find staff members who will earn you more than you will spend on them. It does not matter how much the time is worth to you, if you can't see them making profit. So you need to buy people in based on red-to-black economics.

Recently I learned of a fantastic idea for buying people's time, talents, skills and knowledge. Use online freelance websites. The best examples are elance.com, guru.com, rentacoder.com and fiverr.com There are skilled people and businesses on there that are capable of providing a wide variety of services for you from wherever they happen to be located, communicating with you via the Internet. If you've got administrative tasks or roles, these are fantastic websites.

I suggest you read *The Four Hour Work Week* by Timothy Ferris. He expressed the idea of using what he called "virtual assistants." These are assistants that you would buy from another company for very little money by western standards, and they would do all the finicky "donkey work" that you just did not want to do, for virtually no money. Look into virtual assistants. I would suggest reading Ferris's entire book, actually. Buy time from people at a rate far less than the value that they create for you so that you make money on that time spent.

Once you have a method for valuing your time and you know what you want to get done, buy the time of others at a cheaper rate. Buy it by hiring staff or virtual assistants. This allows the additional possibility of setting up a completely virtual-style business in which you would get all the work done through outsourcing, eliminating the need for a central location.

Time management is very, very important. Some resources I would suggest for you to help get control over your time and get the most out of your time are: *No BS Time Management* by Dan Kennedy, *The Four Hour Work Week* by Timothy Ferriss. I also give a few methods of time management over on the SnowHow blog www.thesnowhow.com so do check that out.

There was a very famous copywriter by the name of Eugene Schwartz. In an interview he talked about breaking your time down into units. He used to break his time into units of 33 minutes, and he would completely focus on whatever he was doing for 33 minutes, allowing no interruptions or distractions. After 33 minutes, he'd take a little break, and then he'd go at it for another 33 minutes. Well I've adopted this strategy and I've accomplished an awful lot because of it. However, I don't use 33 minutes, it seemed a tiny bit too long for me. Instead, I use time increments of 27 minutes. I work with extreme focus for 27 minutes. I completely concentrate on what I'm doing for 27 minutes and once that unit of time is ended, I stop. It doesn't matter where I am in my work. Whether I'm in the middle of a sentence or an action, I stop.

I use a countdown timer for this. You can find countdown timers anywhere. Buy one at your local shop. Most mobile phones have a countdown timer on them so you can use your mobile-timer. On my mac I use an app called the Alinof timer (it's free). Program in 27 minutes or whatever you find is your maximum amount you can concentrate before your mind starts to get tired or your focus starts to wane. Use that time with pure, unadulterated focus, energy, and non-interruption. You'll find you'll get unbelievable amounts of quality work done in these time slots. After the stopwatch goes off, take a short break. Stand up and stretch or go for a cup of coffee. Maybe just have a glass of water. Whatever you choose to do for your short break, make sure you're stepping away from your desk or from your workplace. Take between 3 to 10 minutes, and give your brain time to relax. Then you can get back to doing whatever you were doing in a focused and reasonable manner. I would argue if you can get 4-5 of these segments in your day you will get more done in this time than most people get done in a whole day.

If you are going to use your own time, do it in the most effective manner possible. Time management strategies will allow you to both understand how to use and value your time and also use and value other people's time.

Humble Yourself

Other people's work is a very similar concept to other people's time. You are looking to delegate all the work that you're not good at, that you don't like to do, that you can get someone to do better than you or more cost-effectively than you. When you start out a business, sometimes you have to do all the work yourself, and that's fine until you can start to delegate the work. Once you can afford to delegate, do so. One of the big mistakes I've had in my business career is that I've always wanted to do everything myself, and I've always thought that I could do everything better myself. This has always held me back, and maybe I could have been in a far greater position than I am if I had learned to delegate work.

Most people would happily be where I am, but I would have gotten far further far faster if I had developed my delegation skills. I'm not the best delegator in the world. I recognize this as a weakness in my arsenal, as it were, and would recommend that you learn from my mistakes. Learn to delegate as much work as you humanly can, because you will get a faster and often better result by delegating than by not delegating.

The only times I would suggest that you don't delegate work are in times of crisis. If you've got some big problems to work through, take the work on yourself because no one will be more focused or try harder to get the work done than you will. So don't delegate in a crisis, but do delegate generally. When a new employee starts out, you will be delegating them work that you know you can do better than they. At the start maybe they're only going to be about 40% as good at the work as you. After two months, maybe they'll be 60, 80, or maybe 90% as good as you would be at the work. After 3 or

4 months, because that one task is the only thing they're focusing on, usually they'll be 120 to 130% as good as you are at that work.

So delegate all the tasks that aren't the most forward essence actions, those that aren't most effectively utilizing your time. Look for the best use of your time, the ones that earn you and your business the most money. Focus solely on that, and then look to delegate any work that doesn't fall in line with your best efforts, your best ability. When you are looking for resources, always look at other people's, not just your own.

Chapter 11

Bringing to the Market

Let's talk about bringing your product to market. The earlier section about finding your starving crowd is an excellent introduction to this chapter. You may want to briefly review it before reading on. As I mentioned there, when you're looking to bring your product to market, you should have already asked the questions, "Where is my starving crowd? What do they want? How much will they pay?" You will also have tested various scenarios about your methods of getting to your customers. You will have made sure that they are easily reachable.

The first part of bringing your product to market is this- *concentrate on selling*. To many people "selling" and "salesmanship" are ugly words. They are disgusting notions and shouldn't have to be done. If the product is so good, and most people believe their products are, it should sell itself on its own merits. Again, you don't want to fall victim to the *Field of Dreams* trap. An awful lot of businesses fail due to that thinking. You will need to concentrate on sales. You will need to bring people to your business and you will need to sell your product. If you don't, I'm afraid that you will, or at least the majority of people will, end your business with failure.

One Down

When starting a business, the most important question to ask yourself is, "How do I make the first sale?" Now, if you've gone through the starving crowd process you should know exactly how to make your first sale. In finding your marketplace, you will have already considered the questions that lead to that answer. Now all you have to ask is, "How do I get my market to buy?" If you have diligently done all your research, found out how much they are willing to pay, et cetera, you should really already know this, but you still have to convince them to buy. It is now time to consider what methodologies you will employ to make the sale. There are many formats for marketing and we will discuss them shortly.

Right This Way, Folks

The next thing you need to do is develop what I call your "marketing funnel". You need to drive leads, or customers, to your sales process and convert them into business. Once you start consistently bringing in business and you know that your business model has the potential to work. You need to find your **optimum selling strategy**. This is the strategy that allows you to get your customers, clients or prospects buying your products in the singularly most cost-effective manner. In any business there will be an optimum way of selling that business's product or service. In the previous section on resources, you learned that you need to find out exactly what that strategy is. It may be word of mouth, advertising or one of the other methods I have discussed.

Once you've got your optimum selling strategy, you will need to refine and perfect it so that you can get every single penny out of that strategy.

Take that strategy and use it to its ultimate effectiveness. Saturate your marketplace with your selling strategy. Obtain every single sale you can out of that particular strategy. Then look for your second best selling strategy.

Let's say you were using newspaper advertising to gain your customers, and you did all the newspaper advertising you could as your main strategy until you could sell no more through that strategy. No more newspaper advertisements will help you sell anymore. Now it's time to look for your second selling strategy. Maybe it's face-to-face sales or Internet marketing. Once you find that strategy, and you will need to test the various different marketing methods in order to find it, optimize it until you can sell no more with that strategy.

The reason you need two selling strategies is this: from time to time one of your strategies may lose effectiveness, and you'll be left out in the cold if that was the only strategy you had. *You do not want to build your business around one, and only one selling strategy.* If you build a business around only one selling strategy, and it fails at some point in the future, you will lose your business.

This has happened to businesses before. Just ask anyone who was using SEO (search engine optimisation) before they got "slapped" by one of Googles updates. Some people were so reliant on that selling strategy that they took ages to adjust to the new updates and lost so much revenue because the new rules took a long time to adjust to. Some just could not recover from it. That is why you need both a primary and secondary selling strategy. If something goes wrong with either, you have backup. Once you've saturated your secondary method, find a third method, fourth method, and so on, until you reach strategies that, when tested, are found to be unprofitable.

Again, the most important step in running a business is the first sale. Then the second sale and then, once you're making a consistent amount of sales, ask yourself, "What is my optimum selling strategy? What is the best ways to bring customers in?" Without sales, your business will not go and grow. Prove you can sell. If you don't feel you have the skills to sell, I'll talk later about what you can do to get around that.

Various Methods of Marketing, Sales and Promotions

After answering the questions, "Where is my starving crowd? What do they want? How much will they pay? How do I make my first sale?" you will already have an idea of how to market to your customers. This section will give you some ideas and strategies about different methods of getting to your customers. This is a reasonably small section. You won't get a whole unadulterated course in salesmanship and marketing here. What you will get are some ideas and directions as to where to go for further information on these things.

The first strategy that many people use is face-to-face selling and really this is a good plan ask someone if they want to buy what you have. If you can't make a sale you don't have a business. This method is quite common in business, be it retail, business-to-consumer or business-to-business. Face-to-face selling is a standardized method. There are various methods of becoming good at face-to-face selling. Two books I would recommend on the subject are *How I Raised Myself from Failure to Success in Selling* by Frank Bettger and Neil Rackham's *Spin Selling*, for larger ticket sales.

Selling is an ugly word with some people but it is essential part of all business. You should spend time to master this skill and anyone can become "a born salesman or have "the gift of the gab" with some study and a lot of practice. So get to it.

The next strategy is advertising. Advertising can be done using various formats but we will divide them into two for ease first

Offline/traditional: newspaper, magazine, TV or radio advertising etc. Online: SEO, ads (Facebook, Google), Social media (blogging, twitter, Facebook etc) If you are going to go down either of these paths, an you will need an understand that advertising is a very specialized field and you will need specific knowledge for advertising. I recommend you learn copywriting and other salesmanship skills. Copywriting is one of the three great financial leveraging skills. Copywriting, salesmanship, and marketing are the three skills that really allow businesses to go and grow.

Advertising, I believe, was originally called "salesmanship multiplied" and that is exactly what it accomplishes when done correctly. If you are a new business, one of the things you really need to steer clear of is what's called "institutional advertising." This kind of advertising does not require people to take action. If people want to sell you mind awareness, brand awareness and creating a brand, stay away from these people. If you are a big corporation of have an unlimited budget, you can afford to employ those strategies. If that is not the case, what you're likely looking for when advertising is something called **direct response**.

Employing direct response advertising means you put out a sales message and people either respond to your sales message or they don't. Follow that method rather than institutional advertising because you can track it, test it, assess it and see how it's working. If you just put out a standardized message saying something that seems artsy or cutesy or fun, but doesn't say anything that will deliver sales to your business, you are wasting money. So stay away from people who want to talk about brand awareness and institutional advertising. It's not that these are routes that you can't ever take, but when you are starting out, you want to employ **direct response** advertising. This will allow you to see that your advertising is working. I can't teach you the basis of direct response advertising at this moment in time, but I will give you directions in the next part of the section that will allow you to learn about this.

Sometimes people in business will bring consumers in with a product priced to where they know they will lose money. They also know, however, that they've got a good back-end product or something else that they can sell. So they offer their initial product or services at a cost far lower than someone elses, knowing that the lifetime value of that customer will far outweigh the initial loss that you take in order to gain that client. (Understanding the lifetime value of a client is the number one thing you need to find out about your business after your discover your optimum selling strategy) This is a classic example of the lead generation system. If you are looking for ways of getting people into your marketing funnel or process using a low cost strategy or budget strategy can be effective.

The final method of obtaining leads, and probably the best of all is what is known as joint ventures or host-beneficiary relationships. Whenever you develop a product or service, if you're not the first in the marketplace, there is someone who already is. They have a relationship with customers that you want to reach.

Let's say you are starting a beauty salon and just around the corner from you there is a hairdresser's. Now the hairdresser doesn't make any beauty products, and you don't cut hair. If you went to the hair dressing salon and said, "Look, you have a customer list of a couple of hundred customers who are ideal prospects for me, so if you send a nice message to them saying that we've opened up and will give a discount to your clients, we'll give you a percentage of the profits that we get from them." Why give them a percentage of the profits? First of all, you get an instant stream of quick customers to you, without having to pay any other marketing expenses. Also, if a person a customer already likes, respects and does business with recommends a product that they would be interested in, the probability of that customer doing business with you is far more likely. Look for businesses with symbiotic products that aren't in competition with you.

There are other symbiotic relationships you can form. Say you see someone who is selling a product that's similar to yours, but they've got a one-sale deal. Let's say they're in the auto sales business. They generally sell only one car to their customers. Once their customers have bought one, they tend not to buy a second car from them for at least several years. Go to that person, and say, "Hey, look, I've got an anti-theft security system that you can sell to your customers, so if you sell my product I'll give you a percentage of the profit. That means you get more revenue out of every customer who comes through your doors. In this way, once you've made your sale you haven't reached the end of your sale cycle."

In creating joint ventures, you should be looking for people who already have a list of customers, or even distribution channels. If you can put your products in other people's businesses, and they sell them for you, you've cut out your need to drag customers to your business.

There is also a concept called an endorsed relationship to a champion circle of influence. By way of explanation, imagine I said you to you, "Look at my business. This is the best business in the world and you should come and do business with me." You are going to be very skeptical. You are going to have some initial suspicion, whether you like my product or not. Even if you are looking for the product I am selling and are prepared to actually buy my product or service, you will be slow to trust me. But, let's say you already have a relationship with someone else who you like, trust and respect. If that person were to say, "Oh my god! I know someone, and they've got the greatest product or service in the world, and you should do business with them." You will be far more likely to actually believe that person and do business with me.

An endorsed relationship to a champion circle of influence cannot only get you past the need for credibility, but it can also deliver to you a very large stream of qualified prospects without the need for you to find them one by one. Think about joint ventures as a method. Ask yourself, "Who's already got my customers, and would they be prepared to sell *my* products or service too?"

Learning from the Masters

When I started out learning to be an entrepreneur, I picked a lot of people's brains. Find other people who have knowledge and experience and pursue conversations with them to gain all the best ideas. I realized while working on some of the businesses that I was growing that I didn't know everything about the marketing and promotion of that business. So I asked the question, "Who are the best marketers and promoters in the world? How can I learn from them?" I went out and I found the answers to these questions.

When I was doing my research, a few names kept on popping up. The first of these was a gentleman by the name of Jay Abraham. He is what you would call a "legend" in the marketing world. So many modern day marketers have gotten their start by learning from him, either by being his mentees or simply learning his strategies and tactics from the resources he has made available. Jay is, in my opinion, a bona fide genius. Jay put forth an awful lot of the ideas that are standardized within many different communities, both online and offline. He is well respected. If you want to learn directly from Jay Abraham you can go directly to his website, abraham.com. He also has a book available on his website (the first chapter is free) called *Getting Everything You Can Out of All You've Got*. It's a book you can get for only a few dollars/pounds, and it's worth every single penny you pay for it and more. In fact, I've said to many people in the past that if you want the quickest and fastest way to get an unbelievable business education, I would suggest you read just that one book. That book will give you an understanding of how to get clients and outperform your competition better than would any other book that I've ever read.

I've gone through a lot of Jay's other courses on marketing including his audio-tapes. He does occasionally give seminars ranging in price from a couple thousand dollars all the way up to $25,000. If his pockets aren't that deep, you can find his products online, look on eBay. I can't tell you how much the information is worth.

The next person you need to learn from is a gentleman who has unfortunately recently died. He is the late, great Gary Halbert. Within any industry the word 'genius' gets bandied around quite often. On many occasion the title isn't well deserved. Gary Halbert *was* a true genius. He had an unbelievable, creative clever mind. He was a fantastic copywriter. He created the best sales letter ever written, the Coat of Arms letter. It is apparently the most-mailed letter in history.

Gary offered up an awful lot of advice. He put out a newsletter, usually once a month, and because of that newsletter, an awful lot of people made and awful lot of money. It wasn't just a newsletter about copywriting; it was a newsletter about making money in general. The beautiful thing is this: when the Gary Halbert newsletter was being regularly published, people paid thousands of dollars for subscriptions. Now there is a website that holds the majority of his newsletter archives and you can go and have a look at them for free. The website for that is thegaryhalbertletter.com. Start at the bottom and work your way up, you will get one of the most brilliant marketing and business educations that you are ever likely to get. His newsletters are a fantastic, unbelievably free resource.

The next person I would suggest you learn from is a gentleman by the name of Dan Kennedy. Again, he is a mentor to many of the modern Internet business gurus. If you can get any of his material then do so. He has sold millions of dollars worth of his fantastic course *Magnetic Marketing*. I believe you can find it on his website, or if you're looking for some cheaper options, Ebay. He also has two books, *The Ultimate Sales Letter* and *The Ultimate Marketing Plan*. Take a look at them. He also wrote the *No BS* series of books that are truly awesome. I would suggest that you get the whole series, they are well worth the ten or 15 pounds or dollars that they cost. Start by reading *No BS Sales Success*. Continue with the rest of the series and you will gain unbelievable knowledge from them.

Some other books I would suggest are old classics. *Ogilvy on Advertising* by David Ogilvy and John Caple's *Tested Advertising Methods*. As I've mentioned, one of the great lessons of marketing is to test everything. In business, "test, test, test" is the equivalent of property's "location, location, location." You need to be testing everything. When you read John Caples book you'll realize he's done a lot of the testing for you. This is a resource that can save you time and money.

There's a fantastic book that Jay Abraham has said made him multi-millions of dollars and that he keeps on reading and re-reading. It's called *Scientific Advertising* by Claude Hopkins. I believe you can get a free copy of that online, so do so. Alternately, get it on Amazon in book format. It comes along with another book, *My Life in Advertising and Scientific Advertising*. Again, well worth the small investment.

Another book that you should read is not about marketing, but nonetheless very important. It's about systemizing every approach within your business. It is by Michael Gerber, called *The E Myth*. There's also *The E Myth Revisited,* which is an updated version of his thinking. Read these books. They are fantastic. He will explain how you can systemize a business so that you can turn it into a business rather than a job. Systemizing equals expansion. A business that is well systemized is also easier to sell. Some people are so involved in their business that they can't sell it, because they *are* the business, but a systemized business can easily be transferred from one owner to the next.

The Internet Guru

There are many "gurus" of the Internet marketing world. Discerning which ones are fakes and which have genuine advice to offer you can be tricky. All I can tell you is what I've learned from people I like, trust and respect, whose information I've used to make money. Look these people up online: Frank Kern, Eben Pagan and Ryan Deiss.

Every bit of information I've gotten from Frank Kern, including his free newsletters/videos, has been fantastic. He has courses out there, and I recommend taking them. More importantly sign up for everything that he puts out just to look at his marketing strategies. He comes across as a hokey everyman but inside his head there is a razor sharp making brain. So watch and learn from everything he offers. The same can be said for the others each of them is a goldmine of information and should be learned from.

There are other marketers out there that may be worth learning from, but these are the ones I know and who's information I trust. They may be able to refer you to others, but I can only tell you about the ones I've used.

I have here recommended quite a bit of information for you to look at. This may seem overwhelming, and that's fine. I don't expect you to learn everything at once. In fact, if you recall the section on other people's time, you can find people who are great at selling, marketing, promotion, internet marketing, search engine optimization, lead generation, building lists, building websites, or any of the other skills you don't have but could use for your business. Hire other people to do these things for you. You can hire someone in the real world on a commission basis where they have to make you money or sales in order to get paid. Alternately, go online to a website like elance or rentacoder and hire people who are prepared to provide these services for you cheaply.

Doing the research I have recommended will give you a great advantage over most of the people in your industry who are too lazy or not informed well enough to do so. If you find anything too cumbersome or too time-consuming to do yourself, outsource.

Chapter 12

Failure

Before we finish up, I want to talk about failure. Failure happens in business. I've set up this course and my process has been designed so that if you follow the system, you will eliminate much of the risk involved in getting any business going and growing. That's not to say failures won't happen. A lot of people who face failure say, "Oh my god, that's it. I've reached the end of the road! It's the end of the world! I've tried my best at entrepreneurship and failed!" Other people think, "I've only got one try at entrepreneurship, so if I take that shot and miss, it's all over. I'm doomed and stuck wallowing in the freakish misery that is employment for the rest of my life." I want to tell you that neither case is true.

The Big If

Most people have unreasonable expectations about both being in business and failing at business. They project into the future and they worry about all the 'What ifs?' What if it all goes wrong? What if doesn't work? The weird thing about failure is this: you only fail, at business or at anything in life, *once you stop trying*. If you consistently continue to move forward and progress, every failure that you have along the way is not a failure, but a learning experience. The more learning experiences you have, the better you become.

Often, people who are worried about failure are worried about going into business and having things go wrong. I suggest that even before you go into a business, you should be prepared to fail. Go in *prepared for failure*. Don't think that you only have one shot at entrepreneurship. Go in with the idea that no matter what happens in this first venture, you're going to give yourself 15 to 20 shots at starting a vehicle that's going to get you exactly where you want to go. Your goal may be financial freedom, it may be succeeding just enough to work for yourself or it may be being the richest man in the world.

If you have decided that you only have once chance to succeed at this, and your first endeavor goes wrong, then that's it. Your business life is over. But if you decide to give this as many goes as it takes in order to get where you want to go, failure is not such a horrible prospect. You have 'outs,' as they say in poker. You've got more than one chance to get there.

Fear

Don't ever let fear of failure get in your way. Fear is nothing but a False ExpectationAppearing Real. Fear is often the reason why too many people don't even let themselves try. They fear to start because they don't know exactly where they are going. They think that if they start and get it wrong people are going to laugh at them, and they're going to feel bad about themselves. That just is not the case. I myself have tried and failed in many businesses, and like I say, all you may need is one good business experience in your life to reach financial freedom.

I set up this system to take away much of the risk involved in entrepreneurship. Even with that in place, though, there is still a possibility that you will fail. Accept that possibility. If you allow that possibility to exist while understanding that it's not the end of the world if it happens, you will eliminate a lot of unnecessary pressure you put on yourself. So go into a business with the expectation that it may or may not work out the way you want it to, and if it doesn't, so what? You have at least learned something. With the system we've set up, you've always got other chances.

Falling Up

When I fail, and I have many times, I make sure to make the most out of it by "failing forwards." I learn from my experience, and then I pick myself up, dust myself off, and continue onwards. Don't have an unreasonable expectation about success in business. Realize there is a possibility that things will go wrong, accept it, but know that's not the end of the deal. Don't let the fear of starting paralyze you.

It is actually better to start something and fail than not to start at all. You can take the knowledge from your first experience into your next endeavor, and the one after that. The only guaranteed way to fail at entrepreneurship is by never ever getting started. Don't put yourself in that bracket. Be prepared to fail, and be prepared to fail forward.

When you expect failure, success can be all the more rewarding when it comes. It may happen for you the first time. You may go out there and start a business that goes booming and you get everything you ever wanted in life on your first attempt. That has happened for some lucky people, and for others it takes five, ten, twenty, fifty goes. Ray Krok, the man who developed McDonalds into the great success it is, was 52 by the time he had gotten into his full entrepreneurial stride. It's never too late, there are always going to be opportunities out there.

Failure is an integral part of business. It happens. Some business ideas just don't work out. Accept that possibility. That may never happen to you, you may be one of the lucky ones, but if you're not, don't panic about it. You always get more than one chance. Don't let fear paralyze you: get started. Take action.

Chapter 13

Action

Action is probably *the most important part of this course*. You now have all the knowledge and all the skills you will require to get a business venture off the ground. You have an understanding of whether it's the right time for you. You will be able to find your market. You will be able to develop ideas for your market. You will be able to find the resources to get your idea off the ground. You will know how to bring it to your market. Hopefully, after the last little section, you will also not be worried about starting.

However, there is an awful a lot of information, and a lot of people will get overwhelmed by the sheer amount of stuff they have to do. If you feel that way, it will paralyze you, and stop you from even starting on the entrepreneurial path.

First things first. You've probably gone through this course once. Maybe you need to go through it 2 or 3 times to get a better understanding of everything. Maybe that's the first action you need to take. At some point, you have to take action.

Having Dumbo for Dinner

There's an expression that poses the question, "how do you eat an elephant?" The answer to that question is "one bite at a time." If you try and swallow the whole thing all at once, you will never ever eat that elephant and you will absolutely die in the process. It's just like that with entrepreneurship. If you try to do everything all at once, you will probably be too overwhelmed to get started.

Reverse engineering is the process that will help you get into action, one step at a time. This process involves the micro and macro aspects of the business model. Instead of being scared of the enormity of your whole task, you should break it into sections. You want to look at each section, and break that section down into the easiest and smallest tasks it requires. Just concentrate on doing one little thing at a time. Take on each section individually. Complete the important processes within that section first and move from there. Don't try to do the whole thing at the same time, because your stomach isn't elephant-sized.

Tax Form Evasion

I'll give you an example of how this works. The first time I ever filled out a tax return, I looked at it all the way through, and I thought, "Oh. My. God. I don't understand this. I don't know how to do that. I'll never get this done." And so I left it untouched for a couple of days.

The next time I looked at it I thought, "Hold on a second. Tons of people fill out tax returns every year, so let's just take another look at it." I put the form down in front of me and I started at the very beginning. It asked for my name. I knew how to answer that question, so I filled out my name. Then it asked me for my address, and I knew how to fill out that section. Then it asked me for my date of birth and national insurance number and slowly but surely as I worked through every small section one at a time I was able to answer the questions. Lo and behold, an hour or so later, the form was completed.

When I had initially looked at the tax form as a whole, it seemed too complex for me to complete. So I didn't get started. But once I broke it down into its component parts, I was able manage the task. I would suggest you do the same as you go through this entrepreneurship system: break it down one section at a time.

The Big Picture

If you are a universal or "big picture" thinker, the reverse engineering process may be unnecessary for you. If you are able to grasp the whole course at once and begin accomplishing your goals, then do so. Most people, however, will need to break down the course into manageable portions, or small bites.

Reverse engineering is a great way to get started on your large task. Once you complete the micro system and take care of the smallest individual pieces, the whole, or the macro system comes together on its own. The important thing is this: If you are going to eat your elephant, make sure you take one small bite at a time.

Don't get scared by the big picture, just get started. Take one small step. I suggest that within the first 24 hours of finishing this course, take one action. That one action might be going through the course again if that's what you feel is the next step you need to take. After you've done that, ask yourself the question. "What one small start can I take right now to get my business off the ground?" You've got to take action within the first 24 hours or you'll just put it off.

Entrepreneurial Inertia

The more little steps you take the more momentum you create for yourself, and with increasing momentum comes increasing confidence. The more you progress, the more you will accomplish forward essence actions that will allow you to develop speed, passion and enthusiasm for what you are doing. Other people will find your passion and enthusiasm infectious and begin to follow your lead.

In order to be effective at all, you have to get started as quickly as you can when you get to the end of this course. Since we are nearing the end now, begin to think of one small action that you can take right away. After that, reverse-engineer each section of the course into small bite-size pieces. Quickly you will have conquered your elephant of entrepreneurship. You will have got yourself going, moving towards your very first meaningful business. Take action. Take action today.

Chapter 14

Final Thoughts

Congratulations! You have reached the end of the course! But it's also the beginning of your entrepreneurial life. I've done everything I can that will allow you to have a system that will get your business off the ground, going and growing, and start producing profits. I've given you every strategy and bit of knowledge I know that will allow you to offset the major risks involved in starting your own business. Hopefully by now you will have taken some action in order to get where you want to go.

That is just the beginning. I wish there was a shortcut for you to the happy ending of having a successful business, but there isn't. As you go and grow in business and as you start out going where you need to go, you will need to constantly improve your knowledge and skills within the industry or sector you choose. I've given you strategies and tactics to be able to make that process as quick as humanly possible. You now know how to find a way of making other people's knowledge your own and using it to get where you want to go.

You have only reached the end of the course, as I said, and the road spreads out ahead of you. You will need to constantly improve your knowledge and constantly improve your skills. Learn everything you can about the sector you are in. Learn everything about the skills you'll need to become the greatest producer of ideas, creator, manager, engineer, or whatever it is that you are doing. Look to become the best at what you do. Look to improve every area and every skill of your business knowledge because that will make you better and more successful. When you build your entrepreneurial muscles, everything then becomes easier. The problems that you will have when you start out will seem insurmountable. Let's say problems are rated on a scale of one to ten. When you start out, a one will seem like a ten, but know that a year or two down the line, that "one" problem will seem much more like a one and the "five" problem will be within your grasp.

The more knowledge and skills you have within your industry, the easier it will be to get past the problems that you will inevitably face. Grow your knowledge and skills. Learn from everyone you can. Buy business biographies. Learn from people who have already gone where you want to go, and that will help you fast-track yourself to where you want to go.

I wish you every success in your future entrepreneurial endeavors. I'm sure this is going to be the beginning of something great for you, and get you started off to where you want to go.

I thank you again for taking the time to go through this course. I thank you for allowing me to be of assistance to you, to help you get where you want to go in your entrepreneurial endeavors. I wish you all the best of luck in the future. Thank you once again. Be well and stay lucky.

-Neil

P.S One final thing, I offer many great ideas and resources for free that deal with not just entrepreneurship, but also winning the game of life over at
http://thesnowhow.com
go check it out there are many ideas on there that will help you.

13676374R00057

Printed in Great Britain
by Amazon.co.uk, Ltd.,
Marston Gate.